(continued from front flap)

These facts — background to the current university crisis — are most significant when analyzed within the social milieu in which they occurred. It is this approach that makes STUDENT AND THE UNIVERSITY unique among other books on the subject. It does more than chronicle student disorder; it traces the growth and development of the university within its broader context.

Fully indexed

———— ◄●► ————

Elvin Abeles, highly qualified encyclopedist, has edited the *Living Encyclopedia of the World, Encyclopedia International,* and *Collier's Encyclopedia.* He is also former Editor-in-Chief of the *National Encyclopedia.*

As author of the featured article "Students Challenge the Status Quo" in the 1969 Year Book *Living History of the World,* Mr. Abeles brings calm perspective and objectivity to a highly controversial subject.

His education includes postgraduate work at Columbia University.

He lives with Mrs. Abeles in Queens Village, New York.

Jacket Design by Larry Ross

Parents' Magazine Press
52 Vanderbilt Avenue
New York, New York 10017

THE STUDENT AND THE UNIVERSITY

A Background Book on the Campus Revolt

By ELVIN ABELES

Parents' Magazine Press • *New York*

Each Background Book is concerned with the broad spectrum of people, places and events affecting the national and international scene. Written simply and clearly, the books in this series will engage the minds and interests of people living in a world of great change.

CONTENTS

INTRODUCTION

DURING THE LAST FOUR DECADES, college enrollment has increased from one million students to nearly seven million. The university structure has become progressively more complex and has already led to the existence of the "multiversity." Under these more concentrated conditions, young persons on the college campus have dramatically protested a power structure that allows depersonalization, racial injustice, poverty, hunger, and war to continue. The students' overt unrest has caused a growing number of citizens to question not only the value of the social and economic institutions against which the students are protesting, but also the relevancy of the university itself.

In light of this situation, a volume that carefully and thoughtfully treats the origin and development of institutions of higher learning is most timely. The author of *The Student and the University* has effectively written just such a volume. Indeed, Mr. Abeles' excellent job of analyzing the current campus scene should be received with appreciation and enthusiasm by all who are concerned with the frustrating problems associated with higher education.

In the first chapter, Mr. Abeles carefully traces the development of organized learning from its earliest beginnings in the feudal societies of Europe. He discusses the rise of the new kind of school known as the *studium* or "study place" as distinguished from the church school known as the *schola*. He shows how the *studium* was developed into a *universitas* during the twelfth century by combining masters and students into a single organization. He describes the evolution of administration in these early institutions and the development of the subject matter to include science as well as philosophy and theology. He shows, somewhat reassuringly, that student tension, unrest and outright rebellion are not of recent origin at institutions of higher learning, but have been commonplace from the beginning.

In the succeeding chapters, the author discusses the development of higher education in the United States. He begins with the "New Cambridge" (the forerunner of Harvard University), which was established early in the seventeenth century across the river from Boston. He proceeds with attention to the eight other colleges founded in the thirteen colonies, and with discussion of the land grant colleges, state universities and private institutions established as the nation expanded westward.

Enlightening attention is given to the evolution of management and administration in the colleges and universities of the new world—general management by lay boards and administration by presidents, in contrast with the European situation where the institutions were largely self-governed and administered by faculty-elected rectors.

The author makes a significant contribution by tracing the increasing interdependence of higher education and the military-industrial complex in the United States, and he relates this to the development of the concept of the Establishment. He relates student unrest to the failure of universities and colleges to adjust to rapidly changing times. The consequence is a failure to provide relevant and useful educational opportunities to the students, who must face certain basic previously unsolved sociological problems that now demand solutions. He relates student violence to the indifference of educational administrators who, for a long time, have heard student complaints but have done nothing about them: the failure of university administrators to recognize that very real problems do exist. On the other hand, he places a measure of responsibility on the faculties, who, in many instances, have recognized the existence of problems but have defaulted their obligation to act because of vested interests and commitment to the Establishment.

The book ends with the thought that the challenge raised by the students has forced the faculties to face the question of whether they will "seize the opportunity to restore the integrity of the universities." Both faculty members willing to meet the challenge and students seeking perspective in raising it will benefit from considering points raised in the account presented here.

George L. Cross, President Emeritus
University of Oklahoma
Past President, National Association
of State Universities

AUTHOR'S PREFACE

THE DRAMATIC SURGE of student activism in the past few years has raised questions and even evoked some answers. One of the most familiar questions is a variation of the parental bromide, uttered in the name of the collective adulthood: "What have we done wrong?" One of the answers, also from a 19th-century scenario, seems to be a trip to the woodshed for the collective youth.

The search for a better answer is undoubtedly being undertaken by educators with impeccable credentials, who have debated for decades about the proper function of the university. Meanwhile, an educational conglomerate has evolved, of which the most conspicuous component is the multiversity, classically described by President Clark Kerr of the University of California at Berkeley.

It is no accident that the current upheaval among the student population began at this same institution. The placards raised first at Berkeley and then on campuses across the nation, eclipsed Kerr's scholarly analyses. It was no longer possible to relegate the issues to the trade journals of the academic profession. As front-page news, the campus revolts received extensive, but rarely perceptive, coverage. The dominant overtones were those of contempt, condescension, or dismay. More serious studies pictured the phenomenon as a problem menacing the adult world. At least one expert found lurid evidence for a theory of social psychopathology.

It seemed to me that it would be useful to examine the relationship between the chronic crises in the universities and the current turbulence on the campuses. The students are angry, and they are making demands. Their hostilities are directed against war, racism, repression, regimentation, hypocrisy, and associated evils of a "way of life" for which the university seems geared to condition them. Whether the target for a specific campus uprising happens to be one aspect of one of these evils—a military commitment of the university, bias in the registrar's office, the assembly-line syndrome—or the total system of higher education, it cannot be denied that the presumed beneficiaries of the educational system are in significant numbers alienated from it.

Moreover, the movement is global, diffusing to Kabul and Istanbul, Belgrade and Madrid, Montevideo and Rio, Dakar and Addis Ababa, not to mention ancient seats of student sedition such as Paris and Tokyo and Rome. This can be traced to the common heritage of all the world's secular universities, ultimately deriving from the relatively casual mingling of scholars on the streets of 12th-century Europe. The essential components of the institution that developed were the students and teachers, but with the accretion of apparatus and the distortion of function throughout the centuries, the institution was inexorably co-opted into the service of whatever establishment held power. The manner and particular features of this metamorphosis varied with the society of which the university was a part. A comparative study of the changing university in various countries—for example, Japan, Argentina, Italy, India, Poland, the United States—would reveal why and how student movements in each, while sharing revulsion for "the system" on one level, differ in emphasis, in style, and in effectiveness.

Such a study was not feasible within the space allotted, and this investigation is confined to the system of higher education in the United States, necessarily beginning with its medieval origins. This system is the most highly developed and the most diversified in the world. It is the first to involve a majority of its youth. It is also the most highly integrated into the nation's fundamental economic and political machinery.

The purpose of this book is to examine the highlights in the development of this institution, with special concern for the role of the student. The reader is entitled to at least one clue as to the author's conclusions: Whatever destruction may threaten the American university is more likely to come from inflexible elements within its structure that owe first allegiance to the Establishment than from the free-wheeling, even anti-Establishment youth of the Movement. It is possible that the abrasive activism of the students may have been necessary to compel adults to acknowledge the gravity of the malignancy afflicting the system of higher education. It is scarcely reasonable to insist that those who sound the alarm must be prepared to douse the fire, and it is absurd to cite them for disturbing the peace.

In preparing this account, the author found the following books particularly useful and recommends them for additional study of the subject:

The Medieval University, by Helene Wieruszowski (Van Nostrand, 1966)

Three Centuries of Harvard, by Samuel Eliot Morison (Harvard, 1946)

The American College and University, by Frederick Rudolph (Vintage, 1965)

Higher Education in Transition, by John Brubacher and Willis Rudy (Harper, 1958)

The Contemporary University: U.S.A., edited by Robert S. Morison (Beacon, 1964)

The Academic Revolution, by Christopher Jencks and David Riesman (Doubleday, 1968)

Revolt on the Campus, by James Arthur Wechsler (Covici-Friede, 1935)

The New Radicals, by Paul Jacobs and Saul Landau (Vintage, 1966)

The New Student Left, edited by Mitchell Cohen and Dennis Hale (Beacon, 1967)

The Berkeley Student Revolt, edited by Seymour Martin Lipset and Sheldon S. Wolin (Anchor, 1965)

Berkeley: The New Student Revolt, by Hal Draper (Grove, 1965)

Crisis at Columbia (The Cox Commission Report) (Vintage, 1968)

CHAPTER ONE

THE EUROPEAN BACKGROUND

IN THE BEGINNING was the scholar—so must start a true account of the university. He appeared on the streets of Bologna and Paris, Salerno and Montpellier, Oxford and Salamanca—all the towns of Europe that were beginning to seethe with new life in the 12th and 13th centuries. Boys and young men, poor and rich, came from every land. They spoke many tongues, but all were able to speak at least enough Latin to receive some instruction in that language. They found what lodgings were available and set out for the place where, they had heard, some famous master could instruct them in the new learning.

What brought about this sudden thirst for knowledge? For centuries, the remains of ancient culture lay moldering in abbeys and cathedrals, guarded and doled out by clerics. The monks and lay brothers were trained to do office ("clerical") work for the Church, and to teach the next generation of their own kind to do the same. Only they and the higher clergy they served needed to read and write. Indeed, any person who was literate was considered in most lands to be a member of the clergy and was

1

entitled to the benefits of clergy—especially protection from civil authorities.

Yet some clerics were a little more than mere clerks—they might actually read a manuscript in order to learn from it or to enjoy it, and might even comment on it. Not that this was encouraged, for all truth was supposed to be enshrined in a limited number of sacred writings. Only when a new manuscript turned up that seemed to have some merit or reputation—a work by Plato or Aristotle, for instance—was it considered necessary to "reconcile" any new idea therein to the established teachings.

By the 12th century the institutions of feudal society had reached full flower, and some of the blooms were strange. The patchwork of baronies and duchies was giving way to strong monarchies in England, France, and the Holy Roman Empire. The teachings of Islam, advancing from the East like a glacier, had replaced those of the Church in Spain, Sicily, and Asia Minor. Now the trend was going against the "infidels." As they were pushed back, it was discovered that treasures of ancient culture, hitherto unknown, had been preserved and nourished in the Arabic libraries, like nuggets in a glacial moraine.

The Church had never held greater power and wealth, and it remained the guardian of all the learning that survived—the old learning long copied by clerks, and also the new learning. The new learning the clerks were unable to copy, because there were not enough clerks and because those who could be spared to do it did not know the Greek and Arabic and Hebrew languages in which many of the manuscripts were written.

Perhaps the greatest change in Europe in this period was

the increase in the number, size, and attraction of towns. Those towns with a continuous history from Roman times grew larger, and many others were founded. They were favored by the kings and the Church, partly because they weakened the nobility, whose serfs were attracted by the advantages and freedom of town life.

People began to move from place to place. This had been difficult when any feudal lord could stop a traveler at will, but where kings were in control, there was safe passage. This freedom of movement meant a great deal to the scholars. In 1158 the Emperor Frederick Barbarossa stated clearly: "They [scholars] may go in safety to the places in which the studies are carried on, both they themselves and their messengers, and may dwell there in security."*

With the towns there arose a new class of people, who became known as the "third estate"—the other two being the clergy and the nobles. These were merchants and craftsmen, whose services were needed because of a rapid increase in population after the 11th century. Feudal relations among the nobles, and also between nobles and their serfs, had long been established—everyone knew his "place." But it soon became necessary to determine the role in society of the third estate, so that its members might be dealt with in an orderly manner.

As a result, there developed a new kind of organization: the guild. All those working at the same craft formed a guild of their own. They then chose one of their number to deal with the authorities—the local noble, or the king.

---

* For sources of quotations not directly attributed, see Reference Notes on page 237.

Eventually, in many places, guilds combined to choose officials to represent the entire town or city. This kind of political organization, known as a commune, became widespread in the 12th century.

Within the communes and the various guilds, the members could be kept under control, and outsiders could be prevented from causing trouble. In general, the more powerful kings favored this development (although most nobles did not) and showed their approval by granting charters to the developing town governments. In northern Italy, these governments became so powerful that they were able to band together and defy the Holy Roman Emperor.

All these new conditions proved to be extremely important to the scholars. First of all, the growth of the Church in power and wealth and its new responsibilities as custodian of the new learning increased the number of posts to be filled by literate people. In addition, a vast establishment began to appear in the royal courts and the communes; entirely new and complicated, it could be administered only by educated personnel. The need arose for lawyers, judges, officials, accountants, stewards, people who could prepare documents, compose proclamations, compile information, or merely write letters.

Some of these skills had provided opportunities for clerics even before this period. In many Italian cities, existing since Roman times, some tradition of Roman law had been maintained; and law was taught in a school at Ravenna as early as the 9th century. The art of the notary could always attract students. Medical skills, probably based on Greek practices that had been handed down for centuries, were taught at Salerno in the south of Italy as early as the 10th century.

But the new learning, much of it from Arab sources, brought new life to the schools of law and medicine in Italy in the 11th and 12th centuries. The flow of manuscripts on these subjects and the high fees and urgent need for their services attracted would-be jurists and physicians to seek an education at the Italian schools. Other schools in turn welcomed scholars versed in law and medicine.

The greater ease in traveling inspired scholars to choose more carefully the course of study they preferred. It was no longer necessary to settle for the nearest abbey or cathedral school and a life of incessant copying, with slow advancement up the clerical ladder as the only career open. This was especially important for the disadvantaged, who could not depend on their families to help them find a lucrative or influential post. Pope Alexander III, in 1179, issued a decree: ". . . lest the poor whose parents cannot contribute to their support lack the opportunity to study and to improve, each cathedral church should provide a benefice large enough to cover the needs of a master who would teach the clergy of the respective church and, without payment, poor scholars as well." This was, of course, in the interests of the Church, which was having difficulty in staffing its growing establishment.

But how about the more ambitious? Now they could, like the serfs, find freedom in the towns. (There was an old German saying, *Stadtluft macht frei*—"City air gives freedom.") They could find the teacher of their choice as well. If they were not happy with one master, they could move on. There was no formal schedule, no entrance examination, no matriculation. This same freedom was available to those who had already learned what they needed from one master; another might be giving lectures in a town not far away. Here is an account of a certain monk of Liège: ". . . instilled with an insatiable thirst for learning, whenever he heard of somebody excelling in the arts, he rushed immediately to that place and drank whatever delightful potion he could draw from the master there."

Wherever famous scholars held forth and attracted a band of eager students, there it was likely that a new kind of school would be set up, known as a "study place" (*studium*, as distinguished from the church school, called a *schola*). This was welcomed by the town, for it meant that more money would be spent there, and—it was soon discovered—the reputation of the institution brought fame to the town. Bologna, for example, was of little importance (although it had existed throughout Roman times) until it became a center of learning; and certainly a country town such as Oxford became known through the university that developed there. However, the *studium*, and especially the students, also brought problems to the town.

Order was of prime importance in the feudal period, and there was no recognized place in the set-up of the commune for the students or even some of the masters. The members of the *studium* were attached to neither lord nor church. They were not members of the commune or of any guild. They had neither rights nor responsibilities. And many of them, footloose, filled with youthful exuberance, often poor and finding it necessary to scrounge or steal for food, were troublesome. From the very beginning, brawls and sometimes riots erupted between the townsmen and the scholars, who dressed in a recognized kind of gown (hence, "town-and-gown" clashes). Some means of coping with the new situation had to be found, and this need set the stage for the rise of the university.

The University Takes Form

As we have noted, the cathedral schools were overwhelmed by the tasks and the new responsibilities imposed by the flood of manuscripts. The printing press was yet to be invented, and the mansucript sheets had to be copied by hand. Someone, moreover, had to sift their content to preserve the purity of established teaching, and to "reconcile" apparent contradictions. Under this pressure it was impossible to expand the teaching staff to meet the influx of students. Yet only those licensed by the Church were allowed to provide instruction.

The demand for instruction continued to grow beyond control. Some masters—as those with licenses were called—left the cloisters for the streets, gathered pupils able to pay a fee, and found teaching space wherever they could. In this way, a *studium* would be formed.

A very remarkable master was Peter Abelard, who entered the famous school at Notre Dame in Paris soon after 1100, when he was about twenty-one years old. Unlike most students of the time, he had absorbed enough of the spirit of ancient learning to take a questioning attitude. Although he was engaged in the task of comparing the accepted dogma with the material in ancient manuscripts, he adopted a novel technique. Citing passages that seemed contradictory to approved material, he set one text opposite another and allowed the discrepancies to appear, without drawing conclusions. This was radical and effective; it can still be observed in his famous work *Sic et Non* ("Yes and No"). Examples of his subject matter are: "That Eve alone, not Adam, was seduced; and the opposite," and "That it is permitted to kill men; and the opposite."

Young people could understand this approach, and when Abelard included it in his lectures, his pupils loved it. He became such a popular teacher that when his own master (for most scholars as young as Abelard continued to study) showed his extreme disapproval, the young teacher formed a new school at Melun, and later at Corbeil. Wherever he went, throngs of students followed. Eventually, he went back to the vicinity of Paris, to a church on Mont Sainte Geneviève. (This is now in the Latin Quarter, but it was then just outside the control of the authorities at Notre Dame.) Although the Church continued to disapprove of his teachings, for a time it was compelled to give in, and Abelard became a master at Notre Dame, attracting thousands of students to the cathedral school. By the middle of the 12th century, Paris had become renowned as a center of learning, and the Latin Quarter had become a kind of campus for the student population.

This situation created a problem for the commune of Paris. A modern historian of the medieval universities, Professor Helene Wieruszowski, in *The Medieval University,* describes what followed:

> As the schools grew and, in a double sense, moved away from the protecting walls of the cloisters of Notre Dame into the heart of Paris, and crowds of strangers from all parts of the Christian world mingled with the citizens in daily life, the question of the scholars' status became a problem for the civil authorities. In France, all students, and, still more, all masters of the church schools were considered

members of the clergy, and enjoyed the privileges implied in this status. Whenever the students presented a threat to law and order (and they did so at all times), Parisian officials meted out punishments of the harshest and most inhuman sort. Often they killed or imprisoned the innocent along with the guilty. Since students' demands for redress of grievances were rarely heeded, they in turn resorted to violence.

A similar problem had beset other groups before, and the only solution had been for such a group to win recognition as a responsible body. Such recognition had to come from both the state and the Church, in order to be completely effective. Precedent had been set by the smoothly functioning guilds. Therefore, the members of the *studium* imitated the guild, taking the Latin word *universitas* (literally, "oneness" or totality, and related to the modern word "union") to describe their group.

Members of the Paris *studium*—combining both masters and students—were functioning as a *universitas* by about 1150. Some 30 years later, a problem arose that gave this scholars' "guild" a chance to prove its worth. Traditionally, those intending to teach had to obtain a license from the chancellor, who represented the bishop. Corruption had evidently entered such transactions, for in the previously mentioned decree by Pope Alexander a clause provided that nobody should take money for granting the license for teaching nor should a qualified applicant be denied the license. But who could decide whether or not the applicant was qualified? Some responsible group of masters would have to be consulted, since no one else was capable of giving suitable advice to the busy chancellor. The *universitas,* of course, was entirely capable. Such consultation became so much a matter of course that the role of the chancellor became purely formal; whomever the *universitas* recommended was licensed. This amounted to a sign of recognition by the Church of the "guild" of masters and students.

Recognition by the state was achieved somewhat more dramatically. In 1200 a typical set-to occurred in Paris, in which some students were killed. Immediately after the battle, the French king, Philip Augustus, forced his provost to swear "publicly in the presence of the scholars" that rights specified in a proclamation (we would call them "civil rights") would be guaranteed to the scholars. Every succeeding provost was bound to repeat the oath that the persons and goods of those at the *studium* would be protected against the civil population. Historians often refer to this proclamation as the charter of the University of Paris.

Although the name "university" was not used in the modern sense for centuries after this event, there is little doubt that the "guild" on which the university was based achieved full recognition at about this time. Some 20 years later there is evidence of a guild code of rules binding on all members. Similar codes were in use among the craft guilds and were evidences of self-government, a most important feature of all guilds. This *studium* code, which showed that the masters had control over students and established a pattern of rituals still in use, had features that appeared in almost all the universities. Here, too, the *universitas* imitated the guild; as the apprentice baker or tailor had to follow rules set by the guild over a prescribed period of time in order to become a master baker or tailor and engage in his calling, so those who hoped to qualify for a teaching license had to go through the equivalent of an apprenticeship.

It must be remembered that this pattern was not followed regularly. Each *studium* had its own rules and traditions. Students might be boys of twelve or mature scholars. The content, and of course the style, of the "courses" varied, although in general they consisted of lectures based on an accepted text. It always required a struggle to introduce "modern" material, but on the other hand a school that featured such material might attract certain students.

A Scholars' Manual, although of a much later period (late 15th century), illustrates the extent of "academic freedom" available and the attitude of the students. The form is that of a dialogue between two students. The "realists" and "nominalists" mentioned were advocates of rival philosophies concerning the nature of matter and ideas:

"Tell me the manner of your university."

"I'll do so gladly. First, they revere the method of the nominalists; if there are any realists, they are not admitted, and they are not permitted to lecture or to hold recitations."

"Why?"

"On account of quarrels; for disputes are stirred up from which enmity arises and hatred is born. But to avoid disputes of this sort they think best to have one method only."

"That is not the right way; for if there were more than one method the students would become keener and more versed and more ready in argument. . . . Indeed, among us there are some who follow Albert, some who esteem Thomas, some who admire the most subtle John the Scot and follow in his footsteps [the references are to

Albertus Magnus, Thomas Aquinas, and Duns Scotus]; and the teaching of all these doctors contributes to the exercise of the understanding."

"To tell you the truth, you have now aroused in me a great desire for study. Nothing is sweeter to me, nothing more enjoyable, than to hear what most excellent men think."

Some of our firm knowledge about the early *universitas* is based on a series of statutes issued in the year 1215 by a papal legate for the Paris *studium*. It prescribed a period of six years during which a student must "listen in arts" —i.e., attend lectures in the traditional "seven arts." These comprised language study (grammar and composition of Latin, in this case) and logic, plus rudimentary "scientific" subjects. The *trivium*, the language-and-logic group, provided some useful information for basic skills, such as those of a notary, but the "scientific" studies, called the *quadrivium*, were in fact based on beliefs hundreds of years old and of no real value. The *quadrivium* did prove somewhat more fruitful in the long run, however, after it was enriched by new learning—for example, Ptolemy's geography, Euclid's geometry, and Aristotle's "natural philosophy."

The minimum age for a master in this arts course was twenty. If a student aspired to teach the more advanced course, theology, he had to study for at least eight years (including five in theology) and be at least thirty-five years of age.

The statutes also refer to examinations. A student was expected to attend lectures for the prescribed period of years, although no attendance was checked. He had to rely on memory, unless he was rich enough to buy parchment on which to take notes. When he felt he was ready to take an examination, he faced a board of masters, engaging in a "disputation" or oral defense of some thesis to prove the extent of his learning. This accomplished, he was formally presented to the chancellor to receive the license to teach, called *licentia docendi*. But he was not considered a master by his peers until he had accomplished another requirement —the *principium* or *inceptio*. This was the equivalent of the production of a "master piece" in a craft guild; to prove his teaching ability the student gave a public lecture before the *universitas*. Thereafter his own master set on his head a *biretta* (our mortarboard), and the young scholar was recognized as a full-fledged master.

This ritual is preserved in the modern commencement, but its original intent—to mark the beginning of the student's career as an instructor—has been virtually forgotten, and it has moreover been set backward to mark the conferring of the bachelor's, rather than the master's, degree. In the medieval university, a bachelor was merely an older student who, a few years before his *principium,* was encouraged to coach younger students. He celebrated the receipt of this privilege—and the rank of "bachelor"—by feasting the entire student body. Except in the United States, the baccalaureate has never been considered a final degree in higher education; in English universities, it became a preliminary degree given after three years, similar to the Associate in Arts granted in American colleges. In modern France, the graduate of a high school (*lycée*) receives a baccalaureate.

In a *studium* that was entirely concerned with the professions, the students were likely to be relatively mature.

In such a case the *universitas,* when it was formed, consisted only of students. They chose the masters, and they
prescribed the hours of teaching and the dress to be
worn. One such *universitas* was that of Bologna. Wieruszowski cites some of its 14th-century rules:

> No doctor of the two laws is allowed to begin his
> morning lecture before the bell at St. Peter's finishes
> ringing for the morning mass; he must be in or around
> the school before; after the bell, he must start lecturing
> immediately. . . . Since we are afraid of absences, we rule
> that no doctor of canon or civil law . . . should absent
> himself beyond the boundaries of the City of Bologna and
> stay away so long that students will either lose a lecture
> or will have to substitute someone else for him; but he
> can do this when he has a plausible reason for such an
> absence and has begged the permission of his students.

The University and Society

Once the university was established, it came to be considered a great asset to the commune and to the country.
At Bologna, for example, the city fathers ordered the chief
magistrate to "strive zealously to secure the permanent stay
at the city of Bologna of the *studium* of civil and canon
law, of grammar, dialectic, medicine, *dictamen* [letter writ-
ing] and of other officially admitted sciences. . . ." The
prompt response of King Philip Augustus in defending
the *studium* of Paris against his own provost reflects the
same concern. There was reason for it. The scholars were
aware of their importance, and since no physical plant
existed—no classrooms, no dormitories, no library—to hold
them within the city walls, they were free to shop else-

where, whether for higher fees as teachers, for superior instruction as students, or for better conditions in which to teach and study.

The most spectacular test came in 1229, six years after the death of Philip Augustus. A tavern brawl expanded into widespread disturbances, and the provost sent in his soldiers. The Church supported the suppression. In response, the *universitas* declared a *cessatio*—the masters simply stopped teaching. When this failed to influence the authorities, the Paris *studium* was completely shut down for a period of years, and the scholars had no difficulty in finding a more friendly campus.

The masters of Toulouse sent out a notice of the opening of their *studium*. After detailing its abundant intellectual facilities, including "lectures on the *libri naturales* [Aristotle's natural philosophy], the books that were forbidden in Paris," their message continued:

> . . . what else would be lacking there? Scholastic privileges? Not at all! You will enjoy an unbridled freedom. Or are you afraid of the malice of the people or the tyranny of a malevolent prince? Have no fear: the generous Count of Toulouse has assured us of sufficient security and has guaranteed our salaries as well as those to be paid to our servants both coming and going. . . .

Some of the refugees from Paris were welcomed at Orléans and Angers. A most cordial invitation came from England's Henry III:

> We are suffering with you because of the considerable tribulations and anxieties imposed on you by the wicked rules of the Parisians and we desire to remedy your situation in all reverence to God and the Holy Church and to restore your liberty. We want your university to know

that if you desire to transfer yourselves to our kingdom of England and to abide there for the sake of study, we will assign to you whatever boroughs and villages you choose and we will provide for your liberty and tranquility in every convenient way pleasing to God and satisfactory to you.

Other examples of migrations of scholars are numerous. In fact, many, if not most, of the universities founded in the 13th and 14th centuries were originally "universities-in-exile." But it is worthwhile to consider the results of an even earlier migration—that of the generation of Paris scholars at the time when their *universitas* was just beginning to take shape.

In 1167, King Henry II of England was in the midst of the famous dispute with the Archbishop of Canterbury, Thomas à Becket, who had fled to France. English scholars then studying in France were ordered home, and those who intended to go to Paris were prevented from leaving England. A *studium* began to form shortly thereafter in a small town northwest of London, where there was no school at all. It is probable, although no one can prove it, that this was the origin of the great University of Oxford. In any case, by 1201 a *universitas* of masters and students existed there.

Soon after this, King John and Pope Innocent III were engaged in a long and serious quarrel, in which the new university became involved. The university and the town of Oxford apparently were at odds from the beginning, and the students seem to have been badly treated under the civil (king's) law, although they claimed the benefits of clergy (Church law). An exodus from the town occurred in 1209, with many of the scholars ending up at the town of Cambridge. The *studium* founded in this way became the University of Cambridge.

Pope Innocent ended the quarrel by humbling the king and, along with him, the town of Oxford, which had taken the royal side. The town was forced to pay a perpetual fine to provide funds for the university and to grant clerical rights to the scholars. This made it necessary for a Church representative to reside in the town, because the nearest bishop's see was far away, at Lincoln. Thus, in 1214, the Bishop of Lincoln, on papal orders, appointed the first resident chancellor for Oxford University.

As matters developed, the chancellor more frequently took the side of the university than of the Church when differences arose. In the end he became head of the masters' guild.

These were the universities, Oxford and Cambridge, to which Henry III invited the refugees from Paris 15 years later—and many of them came.

Of course, the University of Paris was reconstituted after the teachers' stoppage. By this time it included another form of organization, called the "nation," which was merely the rough grouping of its scholars according to the parts of Europe from which they had come. Although some rivalry between "nations" is recorded, for the most part they were harmonious, and "nations" existed in almost all universities at one time. In Paris each "nation" elected its own leaders, known as proctors, and these in turn chose the rector, who was recognized as the head of the university. This system of self-government contrasts with that of Oxford, where the chancellor was the head official. In Paris, the chancellor had only the formal role of licensing the masters chosen by the guild.

The method of the rector's election was remarkably democratic, as shown by a statute of 1249:

> [he is to] be elected in the following manner: the four proctors of the four nations should elect under oath . . . another man—but not the last one in office—as the future rector; . . . they should not be motivated by the former quarrels nor by love or hatred, nor by honor or shame resulting for any of the nations . . . but primarily by the welfare of the whole *studium*. . . .

At about this time, in Paris and at Oxford, an effort was begun to make life easier for the students and also to help keep them out of trouble. Most students lived in rooming houses or inns, but as time went on special "dormitories" were rented by the university, to be used only by students. Those who lived in such lodgings or "halls" could more easily be watched and made to obey the rules, which were very strict. In 1257 the chaplain of the king of France, Robert de Sorbon, provided funds for a special dormitory for poor scholars working for degrees in theology. This dormitory became part of the University of Paris, and the university was often known as the Sorbonne, from the name of the chaplain.

The rules established by Sorbon have been preserved, and they well illustrate the conditions under which students lived in such lodgings. Here are a few of the commandments:

> . . . those eating in their chambers [must] be quiet and refrain from noise so that the passersby crossing the court and the street be not offended and that their fellow-

students in the adjacent chambers be not disturbed in their study hours. . . . All the students shall wear their outer garment closed; they should not have furs of various and gray color or red and green silk trimming on their cloak or hood. . . . No woman of whatever status shall eat with students in their chambers. If anyone does this, he must pay the fixed penalty [a fine].

These ordinances were in effect in 1274. At about the same time, in England, several benefactors began to spend some of their money to help needy scholars. One of them, John de Baliol, responded to a penance imposed by the Bishop of Durham for having "gotten himself drunk with beer, quite contrary to the fair esteem beseeming his rank, and [for having] done other evil disrespectful to the Church . . ." Today he is remembered as the founder of Balliol College. One after another, usually for less colorful reasons, residence halls were organized for poor students at Oxford and Cambridge. At the English universities these halls, which became known as "colleges," soon changed in character. They were occupied not only by poor students supported by the endowments, but also by paying students and masters.

Soon much of the teaching was transferred from the university to the colleges; it was conducted by the resident masters and some of the older students, and a completely new kind of teaching, called "tutoring," became popular. At first students both studied under tutors in the colleges and attended lectures at the university, but later the colleges grew so large that even the lectures were given in college, and students thought of themselves first as members of the college and only secondarily as members of the university. Only the university could grant degrees, however. This has remained the custom in Oxford and Cambridge.

As was noted before, the head of the University of Oxford was the chancellor, but the institution was run by the masters, who elected him. As the colleges grew, they also developed a system of self-government. Certain scholars who were known as "fellows" of the college—originally those benefiting from endowments, and later others chosen by them—made the rules and chose their own officials, whose titles varied (provost, warden, rector, and others). However, there was always one official, intended to represent the founder of the college, who could intervene in its administration at will. Usually a churchman, this official was known as the visitor. This title is unfamiliar in the United States, although the College of William and Mary had a board of visitors. At Harvard such officials were called overseers; a more modern term would be trustees.

The college as a unit within the university did not thrive outside of England. Its most promising development, as it turned out, was far in the future—after it had been transplanted to New World soil—but that is another story.

Thus the two great medieval institutions, the university and the college, were well established by the end of the 13th century, and for another 300 years or so they were the leading centers of learning and culture in most of Europe. In the French and other continental universities, the Church maintained strong control. Scholars tended to turn inward, devoting themselves to the task of digesting each new idea as it appeared. From the time of Abelard, the main effort of the Church was the maintenance of the purity of its teachings, avoiding contamination from the writings of the "pagans," as these came to light. For the development of human knowledge, this was to prove a dead end—yet it was the path taken by the Church and its servants, the universities.

We have already noted that one of the purposes of the medieval university was to train personnel for the royal courts and the communes, and this continued to some extent. The constant wars of the 14th and 15th centuries had their effect on society, however, and the strong monarchies that appeared to be forming in France and the Holy Roman Empire fell apart, the former temporarily, the latter permanently. In many regions, town life and its accompanying activities continued to flourish, and schools below the university level began to appear, especially in the Netherlands. A number of universities also developed from *studia* that were founded by local rulers of varying degrees of eminence.

In England, there was no need for the sovereign to challenge the Church in this area, for when Henry VIII made himself head of the Church of England in 1534, Oxford and Cambridge were at his mercy. It was not long before the chancellor, originally a servant of the Church and later a respected head of a university, had become a figurehead. In the words of John P. Davis, who analyzed the early structure of the institution, he served as the university's "ambassador or advocate, almost the royal minister of higher education, and resident at court, leaving his active work as administrative head to be done by a resident vice-chancellor; he must now be a courtier or courtly prelate. . . ." Oxford and Cambridge "were now used to subserve the interests of the monarchy." When Parliament, early in the reign of Elizabeth I, incorporated the University of Oxford, the state assumed the right to interfere in its internal affairs. Thereafter the universities were weathervanes to whatever royal winds might blow.

Whether under royal or Church control, the universities had by the end of the 15th century lost touch with society. For Europe had changed, and by the time Columbus was ready to "discover" a New World, the old world was beginning to renew itself. The new learning of the 12th century, which had sparked the rise of universities, was outmatched by the Revival of Learning of the 16th century. But this outburst of intellectual energy found the universities sterile and unsympathetic. The scholars of the Renaissance operated outside of the campuses.

Student "Passivism" and Action Off Campus

So we return to the scholar, student and teacher, whose laboratory—the university—we have been examining in some detail. It was the scholars' desire for knowledge that made the university possible. Some wanted to learn for the sheer pleasure of intellectual exercise or curiosity about what was yet unknown. A few, such as Abelard, combined the search for learning with the search for God, and in so doing came near to the spirit of science. It was Abelard who praised

> that type of industrious and frequent inquiry which the most profound of all philosophers, Aristotle, recommended to his students when he said: "It is perhaps difficult to solve such things with confidence unless they have been discussed frequently. It will not be useless to express doubt about some of them." For through doubting we come to

inquiry and through inquiry we perceive the truth according to Truth Himself: "Seek and you will find, knock and the door will be opened to you."

If there had been more Abelards, and they had been permitted to operate freely, the contribution of the medieval university might have been greater. But most of the scholars sought advancement in their careers, and they studied with this in mind. A few were willing to cut corners to achieve their goals, as this dialogue from the Scholars' Manual shows:

"It's rather dull and tiresome . . . to be present all the time. I am afraid I'll never do it."

"But if you want to be promoted you can't avoid it."

"I'll say I was present."

"Then you will be a liar. But you have a healthy complexion and the lie won't show on your face."

For the ambitious, the job seekers, and for the society that required their services, the universities were adequate enough.

But society changed, and the universities, in the tight grip of the Church and the monarchs—the Establishment—did not change, at least not at the same pace. This was no fault of the scholars. As long as they were able, through their guild, to control their own way of life, there was growth and hope. They had brought about the change from *studium* to university. Then they became subject to authorities that impeded their growth. Those who merely sought careers could hardly complain, for their needs were taken care of. But the minority who believed there were other uses for a university—not merely the handing down of traditional learning and the training of personnel, but the expansion of knowledge, intellectual leadership–this minority found no outlet for their ambitions. As a result, the passive majority found a safe shelter on campus and security in the society served by the universities; the others made intellectual history elsewhere. It is the names of these others that are remembered.

The centuries between the period of exploration and the Industrial Revolution (approximately 1450 to 1750) saw changes in the world more stupendous than those of the preceding thousand years. Europeans sailed around the world and then seized and settled vast areas. Armies bearing guns forged competing empires. The material base of society was transformed as precious metals were forced out of the earth, the seas bore more goods than the roads, and wealth left the castles for the counting houses. Above all, minds were bursting with new ideas, age-old customs were shattered, and the printed word liberated learning from the Church and made it available to multitudes.

The first break on the cultural front came in Italy, where a deep-seated reverence for the wisdom of the ancients was stimulated by the large-scale recovery of manuscripts early in the 15th century. Contact with the East during and after the Crusades brought knowledge of the Greek language to scholars, and many of them–we know them now as Humanists–refused to accept the Church's interpretations of what they read. They became especially hostile toward the Scholastics in the universities. Some of the powerful nobles who were becoming leaders in the communes of Italy were also scholars, or friendly to them, and helped them found institutions where their collections could be gathered and their ideas could be taught. These institutions, known as academies, became the centers of intellectual activity in such places as Ferrara and Florence. From them, scholars went north to France and England and Germany, and they introduced ideas about education very different from those found in the universities.

To the Humanist, it was more important to be a well-rounded, wise human being than a competent clerk or lawyer or traditional university professor. Humanist teachings appealed mainly to the aristocrats and the wealthy, who could afford to look beyond the mere job of training and aspire to becoming model gentlemen. But the time was coming when a greater part of the population could share the views of the Humanist scholars.

An illustrious example of the new kind of student and teacher was Desiderius Erasmus, born in Rotterdam in 1466. He attended the University of Paris and was repelled by the teachings of the Scholastics. Erasmus was no educational revolutionary, but he thought clearly and spoke his mind. "I have no patience with the stupidity of the average teacher of grammar who wastes precious years in hammering rules into children's heads," he wrote. "For it is not by learning rules that we acquire the power of speaking a language, but by daily intercourse with those accustomed to express themselves with exactness and refinement, and by the copious reading of the best authors." This attitude was ill suited to most of the universities of his time. But there were new schools outside the universities that were beginning to apply this 16th-century type of "progressive education."

The Protestant Reformation distressed Erasmus, but it

helped break some of the Church's hold over ideas and the way they could be studied. Of course, it also broke the monopoly of the Church and its hallowed teaching apparatus—the universities—and it made men think in a new way, not only about religious matters, but about closely related intellectual matters. Martin Luther was a master of arts from Erfurt University and a doctor of theology and professor at the University of Wittenberg. He used strong language about the universities, calling them "asses' stalls" and "devils' schools." He had some constructive ideas too: "If the magistrates may compel their able-bodied subjects to carry pike and musket and do military service, there is much more reason for them compelling their subjects to send their children to school."

The Reformation brought new life to education outside the universities. In many cities of Europe, regular teaching became possible for the first time for the children of townsmen. Suggestions for universal and compulsory education began to be voiced, and girls were mentioned as possible pupils.

Once the seemingly solid structure of the Church was breached, there was no end to the process of questioning, and a chain reaction began. Not only was the authority of the Church-blessed Aristotle re-examined—all authority, the very notion that there could be an authority, was doubted. The spirit of Abelard returned to haunt the 16th century.

Francis Bacon, after a stint at Cambridge—where he recoiled from Aristotle—took time in a busy life to write a number of books, in which the main point was: observe and experiment, then draw conclusions. (The medieval practice had been the opposite: adopt conclusions, then show how they must be correct.) On the basis of Bacon's formula, it was possible for the first time for real science to thrive.

It is worth noting that in the years when modern principles of science were forming, those who contributed the most did so in spite of the hostility of the Establishment and at great risk to themselves. Copernicus did not dare publish his work, which contradicted Church dogma, until he was on his deathbed. When Galileo, about 75 years later, using new scientific equipment, began to prove the Copernican picture of the universe, the Establishment lost patience. First, the writings of Copernicus were banned —and they remained banned for 141 years (from 1616 to 1757). Then Galileo was forced to continue teaching the old Ptolemaic theory he knew was wrong, and to deny his own theories. This in turn caused René Descartes, who had adopted some of Galileo's ideas, to change his plan to write a book on science and to switch to philosophy; the result was his *Discourse on Method,* which was a valuable contribution to thought, but one less easily attacked by the Church.

Academies, rather than universities, were the centers in which this newest learning was welcome. The kinds of academies that had sprung up in Renaissance Italy, devoted to education of aristocratic youth, gave way to great institutions of scientific research, also called academies—such as London's Royal Academy. But these were devoted, not to the teaching of knowledge, but rather to the task of adding to the store of knowledge—the advancement of learning.

It is no accident that this was also the title of a great

book by Francis Bacon. *The Advancement of Learning* appeared in 1605, when the first academy of science was being founded in Rome. The book carefully examined the current system of education and thoroughly repudiated the style and content of traditional teaching. It also suggested that a new role would eventually be assumed by the modern university—that of serving society by providing facilities for research.

During the 18th century, in the view of historian William Boyd, ". . . the universities throughout Europe had with few exceptions fallen from their high estate as centres of intellectual life." Yet intellectual life was never more vigorous. Its new sponsors and custodians were able to find other centers of activity, and in the end a new kind of university—with new kinds of scholars—was to recover the old role and add new ones. The process began humbly in a land whose existence was not suspected by Abelard.

CHAPTER TWO

THE AMERICAN BACKGROUND: COLONIAL PERIOD

SCHOLARSHIP WAS PART of the Puritan way of life. Many of the gentlemen who made the laws for the Massachusetts Bay Colony were graduates of Cambridge or Oxford, and it was not strange that they began to think about providing an education for their own children so that the new settlement would have proper leadership in the next and later generations. Since the English universities had equipped them to become preachers and lawmakers, they tried to build a school of the same kind in this very different setting. They called it a "schoale or colledge" in their founding law of 1636, but it had little in common with the colleges that, as we have seen, were units of the great English universities.

The English colleges had grown out of foundations, which meant that some benefactor had provided money for the education of a number of students ("fellows") who became the nucleus of a teaching staff, as well as for the buildings in which they lived and studied. Who was to be the benefactor of the "college" in New Town, across the river from Boston? The students at an English college were given instruction not only by the tutoring fellows who lodged with them, but also by eminent masters at the university. The degree that rewarded their efforts and certified their abilities was granted, not by the college, but by the university. Who would teach the students at the "new Cambridge," and who would give them a degree? For that matter, would they need a degree?

Since the "college" was not endowed, the colonial legislature (known as the General Court) set aside £400, half to be available in 1637 and the rest "when the worke is finished." (In the event, the first building alone cost £1000.) A piece of land in New Town between two cow yards was purchased in 1637 and called the "College Yard" —a name still used for part of the campus. New Town itself was hopefully renamed Cambridge. Meanwhile, a ship from England landed at Boston with two graduates of old Cambridge among its passengers. One, who had taught school in England, was Nathaniel Eaton; he was chosen to become "master" of the new college. His shipmate and friend, John Harvard, became assistant minister at a church in nearby Charlestown and watched the budding school with approval. When the young pastor died in 1638, he left half his estate—about twice the amount set aside by the General Court—to the college, which was promptly named after him.

So Harvard had at least one teacher and, in a modest sense, a benefactor. As it happened, Eaton turned out to be an unsatisfactory "master" (he was never called "president"), and it was not until 1640 that Harvard College really began to operate—this time under the guidance of another Cambridge graduate, Henry Dunster, who did receive the title of president. At the same time, the General Court assigned the revenues from the Boston-to-Charlestown ferry to the use of the college.

Dunster and two or three tutors made up the faculty. The freshman class in 1640 had four students; by 1654 (when Dunster was dismissed for a religious deviation) the student body numbered about 60. The average graduating class even a decade later was only seven, and it took 65 years to double the student body.

This was clearly no big operation. But even in Dunster's time, the degrees granted by Harvard were recognized by Oxford and Cambridge. These degrees were the baccalaureate after four years, and the master's automatically granted after three years of a minimal amount of additional study, not necessarily in the college. The degrees had very little meaning, however. Degrees granted by the medieval universities had served to admit their holders to the "guild" of teachers.

No such guild, nor even a teaching career, existed in New England or anywhere in America. For more than 50 years, the colonies had not another college. The three or four tutors, each of whom provided instruction at Harvard for only a few years, were usually young bachelors waiting to secure a pastorate. Outside of the ministry, there was no career that required a degree or, indeed, any formal education.

This raises other questions: Why were nine colleges established in the original thirteen colonies? What part did they hope to play in colonial society, and what part did they actually play? And what kinds of scholars—teachers and students—did they produce?

The First Colonial Colleges

By the first years of the 17th century England had a large class of people with money who had learned (from the Spaniards, the Portuguese, the Dutch, and the French) how to increase their fortunes by taking for themselves the natural resources in the newly discovered parts of the earth. These people—nobles, shoemakers, weavers, grocers, tradesmen of all kinds—usually did not seize land personally. Just as the medieval scholars had learned from the craft guilds how to form a university, so these early capitalists formed "companies," such as the East India Company or the London Company, and outfitted "adventurers" with the permission of the king (who received a percentage). King James I gave the London Company a charter to settle Virginia, and there the settlers planted their church—the Anglican Church—and talked about setting up a college. But the matter of the college was not too urgent, since they could easily obtain Anglican clergy from Oxford or Cambridge. In 1660 the Virginia legislature, the House of Burgesses, voted to create a college, but by that time it was possible to send a boy to Harvard. In 1693 it was urged that education would help the professed objective (after making money) of saving souls; but "Damn your souls! Raise tobacco!" replied the attorney general for the English sovereigns, William and Mary. Nevertheless, Their Majesties provided a charter in that very year. The institution, which was named the College of William and Mary, was not in a position to function as a college until 1729, by which time George II was on the throne, and Yale had ended its first decade at New Haven.

The Puritan gentlemen who settled Massachusetts Bay

Colony were somewhat different from the backers or the settlers of the London Company. The Puritans themselves both supplied the capital and undertook the settlement. Moreover, they included men of means and education for whom making money was not the driving force. Religion was very important in their lives, and their religion differed from that imposed on England by its kings. First Cambridge, then (under the chancellorship of William Laud) Oxford had been barred to those of their faith, for—as the king prescribed—"The Universities are the nurseries of learning and should be free from all factions." This kind of discrimination impelled these gentlemen farmers, merchants, and preachers to uproot themselves from a familiar and usually comfortable environment and join the Pilgrims (a more "radical" and less favored group of similar faith) in the New World.

The Virginians had carried the Anglican Establishment with them; the Puritans fled from it and created their own Establishment, equally strict and self-serving. Perhaps because they had thought their beliefs through for themselves, however, the Puritans had more respect than the Anglicans (by and large) or the devout of the medieval Church for the right of each person to achieve his own "salvation." One was not "born into" the faith, among the Puritans. It was necessary to become personally committed to its teachings, and this required an ability to read the countless tracts and to understand the preachments from the pulpit. This is why scholarship, of a sort, was in fact part of the Puritan way of life.

People of such earnest habits might sometimes commit acts that a later age would disapprove—the banishment of "heretics" such as Anne Hutchinson and Roger Williams or the hysteria of the Salem witchhunt. But their victims did not burn alive (as did Joan at the hands of the Catholics and Servetus at the hands of the Geneva Calvinists). Nor could the Puritans wait a century or so for a good school for their children. And Harvard was not founded merely to provide ministers. "One of the next things we longed for, and looked after, was to advance Learning and perpetuate it to Posterity," wrote a Puritan in 1643, adding: "dreading to leave an illiterate Ministery to the Churches."

Although the Massachusetts Puritans did their best to preserve an island of stable orthodoxy, which accounts for their severity toward such as Hutchinson and Williams, their temperament also allowed for change. After a generation or two, the stern and unbending were in the minority. Some had moved away voluntarily, as did a group to settle the Connecticut Valley. This group did not want their future ministers to train at "sinful" Harvard, and they proposed to set up a "collegiate school" of their own. Thus, after a home at New Haven and a wealthy benefactor had been found, arose Yale College. Its purpose, said the enabling act of the New Haven Colony in 1701, was that "Youth may be instructed in the Arts & Sciences who thorough the blessing of Almighty God may be fitted for Publick employment both in Church & Civil State." And when Princeton was chartered as the College of New Jersey under the sponsorship of another non-Anglican sect, the Presbyterian, its founders announced that they hoped "it will be a means of raising up men that will be useful in other learned professions—ornaments of state as well as the church."

There is no need to give details about the other five

colleges founded before the Revolution: Columbia (then
called King's), Pennsylvania (Philadelphia), Brown (Rhode
Island), Rutgers (Queen's), and Dartmouth. Other sects
were involved, or, in the case of Pennsylvania, no sect at
all. But nowhere was a profession of faith required, as at
Oxford and Cambridge (until 1871), for a student to enter
a colonial college, and some of the colleges failed to specify
a religious test for faculty members. It simply did not occur
to the founders of Harvard, while their tight little island
of Puritan faith was under control, that anyone of ques-
tionable religious allegiance would dare to apply for a
teaching job. They were quite right, of course; but when
a Baptist in 1720 endowed the first chair at Harvard with
the provision that "none be refused on account of his
belief and practice of adult baptism," the burying ground
just east of the Yard may have heaved slightly. It was just
this sort of hanky-panky that had disturbed the brothers
in New Haven.

It was understood, of course, that each college would
provide the kind of Christian education favored by the
sect that had sponsored the college (represented in the
person of its president), and naturally each college attracted
primarily students of that sect. But in no case was it the
overriding purpose of the college to produce clergymen—
48 per cent of Harvard graduates in the 17th century did
not become ministers. Many of them did enter public life,
and few men in public life were not graduates of a colonial
college.

The curriculum was intended to produce a well-informed,
capable elite. It was based solidly on the Cambridge-
Oxford tradition, but limited by local conditions, for there

was not the abundance of learned masters that had been the glory of the medieval universities in their prime. After the first generation of Harvard presidents (all Cambridge alumni), the teachers were home-trained. The president lived on campus and headed the teaching staff—except for Increase Mather, who spent much time in England and more time in his parish, brushing off his critics with disdain:

> Should I leave off preaching to 1500 souls . . . only to Expound to 40 or 50 Children, few of them capable of Edification by such Exercises?

The fact that such a president could hold office may suggest how hard up the Overseers must have been.

The rest of the staff, the tutors, lived on campus with the "children," each conducting an entire class through its four-year career, and teaching all subjects. Classes were small—fewer than a dozen—but the range of knowledge professed by the young tutors was formidable. It included, of course, the language of instruction, Latin, and also Greek, and a smidgeon of their literatures; logic and rhetoric, the better to train young gentlemen to think and speak; some mathematics; and a potpourri called philosophy, which included natural philosophy—the embryonic sciences. The content of the courses was changed only slightly to reflect the new thought and discoveries of the 17th and 18th centuries, but in this respect the colonial colleges were faithful images of their English cousins. It should be noted, however, that Cartesian philosophy was introduced at Harvard by Thomas Brattle, a tutor, in 1687, and that the Copernican theory replaced that of Ptolemy somewhat earlier. In fact, Harvard received a telescope in 1672, and Sir Isaac Newton praised Tutor Brattle's observations of a comet.

Enlightenment Comes to America

A century later, reform was observable. By this time a new swell of intellectual activity was undermining the entrenched systems of thought. Just as the Revival of Learning of the 16th century (and earlier waves of "new ideas") had disturbed settled and prescribed teachings, so in the 18th century Locke and Hume, Diderot and Voltaire, and other lights of "the Enlightenment" began to penetrate even the English universities and the colonial colleges. This was the so-called Age of Reason, an age in which the "common-sense" ideas of the Third Estate (men who dealt in money and business, not courtiers or clerics) became important enough to win some consideration. Freedom from authority, reason as well as (but not instead of) faith, experimentation—these were the catchwords and practices of the Enlightened, who were best represented in America by Benjamin Franklin and later by Tom Paine.

In 1767, seven years before the future author of *Common Sense* was to reach America and preach subversion to the colonials, a foretaste of liberty was given to the tutors of Harvard. They were allowed to teach only those subjects in which they were competent, instead of attempting to cover the entire (now widening) spectrum of knowledge. Locke's philosophy, Newton's "natural science," and such outlandish subjects as geography and English literature had made an appearance. Moreover, science had become a subject of some importance at Harvard, taught by the president himself. He even convinced the General Court that an expedition should be sent to Newfoundland in 1761 to make observations on the transit of Venus—a pioneer scientific expedition.

Yale was also converted to a more relevant curriculum. By 1745 mathematics had become an entrance requirement, and the study of electrical phenomena was at a level that could induce Franklin—the preeminent scientist in the colonies—to entrust one of his machines to President Ezra Stiles for experimental use. Franklin's influence was also paramount in the curriculum of the College and Academy of Philadelphia, which in 1791 became the University of Pennsylvania. Before the Revolution, this institution had a school of medicine and a department of botany. The curriculum at Philadelphia "was the first systematic course in America not deriving from the medieval tradition nor intended to serve a religious purpose," notes Frederick Rudolph in *The American College and University*.

Franklin (who had never gone to college) was a trustee of the Philadelphia institution, and he was largely responsible for its progressive program. The other eight colleges were not usually so fortunate. Indeed, the way in which an institution was run depended almost entirely on the kind of president it had and on his relations with the Establishment, of which he formed a part.

The Governing Boards

The English colleges had been traditionally self-governing. The fellows of each college chose the head (he was rarely called president—usually rector or provost), and although this autonomy was reduced substantially by the arbitrary demands of the king or his spokesman—still, it was traditional. The visitors, who were supposed to represent the interests of the founder, seldom intervened in the affairs of an English college.

This situation could not be matched in the colonies. When there was a "founder," such as John Harvard or Elihu Yale, his endowment became a trifling part of the revenues of the institution; most of these had to come from a large number of public-spirited donors, the sponsoring church, and the "state"—such as the General Court in Massachusetts or the House of Burgesses in Virginia. The charter that set up the institution was always a political document, and it tried to imitate the English example, but failed.

When the General Court voted its first funds for Harvard, for instance, it entrusted the program to a Board of Overseers made up of six ministers and six magistrates; later the Governor, the president of the college, and others were added, to make a total of 21. But this board was temporary, until the College could establish a proper staff of "fellows" who would be responsible for administration. When the charter was finally devised in 1650, it actually provided for a Corporation (English for *universitas*) of this type, comprising a president, a treasurer, and five fellows, all presumably members of the college.

But where were the five fellows to come from? The college had only two or three tutors, as we have seen, very young men with no background for running a college in the English manner. From the very beginning, therefore, outside ministers were made members of the Corporation and, in view of the youth of the tutors and the turnover among them, many tutors were excluded from it. The actual administration of the college was, moreover, taken out of the hands of the Corporation and assumed by the Overseers —of whom only the president was in any way connected with the college. This gave extraordinary importance to the office of president, not comparable to anything in England or in any other country. The college presidency, like the presidency of the nation soon to arise, was a peculiarly American institution.

By 1720, Harvard had grown to a point at which a full faculty of five was possible, and the original plan for a college-centered governing board might have been realized. Nicholas Sever, a tutor of mature years and a former minister, was refused membership in the Corporation and decided to challenge the practice as contrary to the intention of the charter. A protracted legal battle ensued, involving President John Leverett (who upheld the exclusion of tutors), the Overseers (who opposed the exclusion for political reasons), the General Court of the colony, and the Governor. Finally, when a threat was made to involve the king—which nobody wanted—a decision was made against Sever. Obviously, the autonomy of the college was fictitious, as it was in England. As for the ultimate effect, Harvard historian Samuel Eliot Morison summarized it thus in *Three Centuries of Harvard:*

> If Sever [had] won his point, the College would [have been] controlled, as the Oxford and Cambridge colleges still are, by the resident scholars who did the actual teaching. . . . On the other hand, if Leverett [had] won, it [would have] meant that Harvard would be controlled by the President, assisted by a board of non-resident and

usually subservient trustees. This form of college government by President and external trustees . . . has become
the standard American method of university government.

After the Sever suit, the Corporation was more than ever
made up of noncollege members, and after 1780 no member
of the faculty served on the Corporation. This evidently
satisfied the requirements of the Establishment—for the
Corporation, uncontaminated by any representation from
the teaching staff, from this point on became the more
active of the two governing boards, and the Overseers were
reserved for special occasions.

A similar effect was achieved at Yale. At first, a board
of trustees was set up and empowered to choose their own
successors—a system nowadays known as co-optation, and
practiced at such universities as Columbia. All Yale trustees
had to be ministers and at least 40 years of age. In 1745 a
new charter—which is still in effect—substituted as the
governing board a unit known as President and Fellows.
However, the Fellows were not (as they would have been
in England) teachers at the college—they were the same
middle-aged, co-opting clergy who had been called trustees
in the earlier arrangement. Yale was at least spared the tug-
of-war between Overseers and Corporation, and it was
really the Yale model that was almost universally imitated.

The Colonial Student

With control of the college out of the hands of the
teachers, one may well wonder how much influence the
students could have wielded. Most of them came from
nearby, especially after almost every colony had established
its own center of learning. Although the students were

hardly children, they were on the whole somewhat younger than today's college students, beginning their studies at Harvard, for example, at fifteen to seventeen years of age. They represented a cross section of the community comparable to that on campuses in the United States in the 1920's. According to Morison:

> Merchants, magistrates, and ministers furnished the larger number, but there were a good many sons of plain farmers and artisans, as the town and country parsons made it their business to shape up poor but promising lads for "university learning"; and there were now plenty of scholarships and exhibitions to pay all or part of a student's expense.

Alongside this picture of near-democracy must be noted the brief flowering of unashamed snobbery, for in the middle decades of the 18th century the members of each Harvard and Yale class were officially listed according to a protocol of social rank. But after a "proud father . . . complained that his son was placed in the Class of 1772 below a boy whose father had not been a Justice of the Peace as long as he," an alphabetical system of roll call was adopted.

The records do not reveal much about "student power." One curious event was the case of an unpopular Harvard president, Leonard Hoar, a scholar having an unusual interest in science but lacking the human touch. Cotton Mather, who was one of his students, described in his rather crabbed style how his fellows "set themselves to Travestie whatever he did and said, and aggravate every thing in his Behaviour disagreeable to them, with a Design to make him Odious." In any case, there was a demand that Hoar must go, and when he would not, the students

walked out. Soon thereafter, in March 1675, Hoar resigned
and, it is said, died of a broken heart.

The next evidence of student activity in the colonies
was a century later, and again is reported by Morison:

> The earliest recorded College rebellion occurred in the
> spring of 1766 over bad butter at commons [the dining
> hall]. . . . Asa Dunbar (grandfather of Henry Thoreau)
> complained to Tutor Hancock: "Behold our Butter
> stinketh!" He received no satisfaction; and on his return
> to commons with the bad news, the scholars hissed and
> clapped. For this demonstration Dunbar was condemned
> by the Faculty to confess the sin of insubordination, and
> be degraded in seniority. The students then met in Holden
> Chapel and passed resolutions, in pursuance of which they
> walked out of hall at the next breakfast, before "giving
> thanks," gave three cheers in the Yard, and breakfasted
> in town.
>
> A committee of the Faculty examined the Steward's
> stock of butter, condemned six firkins [casks] absolutely,
> and allowed four "for Sauce only"; but the conduct of the
> students was regarded as equivalent to a treasonable com-
> bination against the Sovereign. Corporation met; Overseers
> met, presided over by his Excellency Governor Bernard;
> and both insisted that the offending students must sign a
> humble confession or leave College.

In the end, 155 students did sign a confession and a
promise to behave in future. But two years later there
appeared a "liberty tree" in the Yard, where "students
assembled to pass resolutions and organize resistance"
against something one of their tutors had done. Again
failing to convince the administration, they threatened to
go to Yale! But the affair was patched up by the Corporation, and all was forgiven.

In that same year the seniors voted to give up drinking tea, five years before the Tea Act provoked some of their fathers into dumping that commodity demonstratively into Boston Harbor. The drinking was evidently a contentious act, for its practice gave rise to a faculty resolution in March 1775 that could nobly serve as a plaque to any Ivory Tower:

> Since the carrying India Teas into the Hall is found to be a Source of uneasiness and grief to many of the Students, and as the use of it is disagreeable to the People of the Country in general; and as those who have carried Tea into the Hall declare that the drinking of it in the Hall is a matter of trifling consequence with them; that they be advised not to carry it in for the future . . . that so peace and happiness may be preserved within the Walls of the College whatever convulsions may unhappily distract the State abroad.

A few weeks later, Paul Revere rode, and the tempest in the teapot had become a Revolution.

CHAPTER THREE

THE GROWING REPUBLIC

LESS THAN THREE GENERATIONS separated the American Revolution from the Civil War. During those years a population of about 3,500,000 burst out of their original seaboard states across the Appalachians, occupied almost all the land east of the Mississippi, and began to settle the Plains and the West Coast, becoming a nation of more than 30,000,000. The subjects of an overseas monarch who could grant or withdraw charters at will became the grandfathers of the citizens of the 34 sovereign states of 1861. And in no field was that sovereignty exercised more jealously than in the field of education.

The westward surge and the sense of independence drastically changed the character of the American college and laid the groundwork for the American university. The colonial college had looked backward, toward England, but the college in the growing republic was something new.

The nine colonial colleges fulfilled their purpose, turning out graduates who could capably preach or hold public office, or both, with proper attitudes, good character, and a foundation of basic learning. As never since in the United States, any graduate of any college could converse with and be understood by any graduate of any other college. However much they might disagree, they shared the mutual respect of individuals produced from a common mold. They were certified members of an aristocracy—a plantation and mercantile aristocracy—whose needs were ideally served by the uniform classical curriculum.

The Revolution left the states free to set up institutions of learning without restrictions. In the first decade after independence, charters were given to eight institutions: three in Virginia, two in Maryland, one in Pennsylvania, one in Georgia, and one in South Carolina—and note, none in New England. In the second decade, another eight charters were awarded, and this time New England fared better, with two to Massachusetts and one to Vermont. North Carolina led with three, and Pennsylvania and New York each received one. Most important, three of the charters (one granted by Virginia, two by North Carolina) went to institutions west of the mountains, in districts that would soon become the new states of Kentucky and Tennessee.

This was a modest beginning, although twice as many colleges appeared in these 20 years as in the previous 150. Actually, although the charters were new, some of the institutions were not.

The New Colleges

Alongside the nine venerable colleges, a sizable group of seminaries and academies had been developing to serve the boys in the colonies who lived too far away from Cambridge or Williamsburg to make the trip. Some of the academies were what would now be called prep schools, providing enough Latin and social graces to open the doors of the more formal colleges—a task otherwise left to educated parents, hired tutors, or nearby ministers. Came the Revolution, and several of the academies emerged as colleges, just as colleges were soon to emerge as universities. Since there were no generally accepted standards, any of these institutions, once chartered, could grant degrees.

For example, the Kent County School on Maryland's Eastern Shore, founded in 1706, became Washington College in 1782, adopting the name of its benefactor, George Washington. For the same reason Augusta Academy in Virginia's Shenandoah Valley, founded in 1749, became Washington Academy after the Revolution and Washington College in 1813; its present name of Washington and Lee University was adopted in 1871—but it is a university in name only. Transylvania Seminary, so named because it was established in Virginia's Kentucky County "beyond the mountains," held its charter for 18 years before it was renamed Transylvania University in 1798. It was controlled successively by the Unitarians, the Presbyterians, and the Disciples of Christ. Long after its medical and law schools, which had justified its university status, had atrophied, the institution gracefully acknowledged that a more suitable name was Transylvania College.

And so it went: no great planting of brand-new institutions in those early years, but a gradual elevation of status, at least in name and degree-granting powers. This was true at least for the private colleges, but a new phenomenon was about to appear—the state university.

Historians still dispute whether Georgia or North Carolina

had the first state university. The University of Georgia was
chartered in 1785, but at the opening of the 19th century
its future site, grandly named Athens, was still unbuilt.
Thirty students and the town materialized in 1801. The
University of North Carolina, chartered in 1789, is reported
in the history books and travel guides to have opened in
1795, thus qualifying as the "oldest state university." What
really happened is described by historian Rudolph.

> On a cold drizzly day in January 1795, a two-story empty
> brick building that called itself the University of North
> Carolina was opened to the public. A bitter wind and an
> unsightly landscape of tree stumps, rough lumber, and
> scarred clay greeted the governor, who had wanted to be
> on hand for the important event. He was also met by the
> faculty, which consisted of one professor doubling as presi-
> dent. A month later the first applicant for admission
> knocked at the door.

These events illustrate most of the trends that were to
appear in the coming years and dominate the educational
scene. There was to be a parallel growth of private and state
degree-granting institutions, using a number of names—academy, college, university—that were never defined. The older
colleges were trying to improve the quality of their educational offerings—by increasing their teaching staffs, by cautiously introducing new courses, by putting aside their sectarian slant. But the newer institutions tried to solve another
problem, that of making education more accessible to more
people. They moved with the frontier, weakly echoing in the
19th-century backwoods what Harvard had done in the Massachusetts backwoods of the 17th century and what Yale had
done in 18th-century Connecticut.

As Rudolph notes, "College-founding in the nineteenth century was undertaken in the same spirit as canal-building, cotton-ginning, farming, and gold-mining." First a church was built, then a general store, and soon afterward a college. Almost every state admitted to the Union before the Civil War was granted land by the Federal government to endow a "university." (Exceptions were Texas and Maine, states in which the Federal government had no land to dispose of.) Generally, when the land grant had been made and a board of trustees set up, the government (Federal and state) let the university make its own way. As a wave of religious activism followed the less devout generation of Franklin and Paine, public interest turned from the creatures of the state to schools set up by the various denominations.

Decision at Dartmouth

In the colonial period, the denominations had learned to coexist, and the boards of trustees were often interdenominational, reflecting the composition of the faculty and the student body. But after the Revolution, with charters easy to obtain, bitter rivalry and destructive competition developed. The Presbyterians and the Congregationalists were the most aggressive, but they were matched by the late-blooming Baptist and Methodist school raisers. They might disagree on dogma, but any one of them could subscribe to part of an early-19th-century Methodist report issued in Indiana:

> . . . we think it very desirable to have an institution under our own control from which we can exclude all doctrines which we deem dangerous. . . .

A boom in crossroads campuses was set off by a United

States Supreme Court ruling in 1819. Fifty years earlier, on the eve of the Revolution, George III had granted a charter to a Congregational minister, Eleazar Wheelock, to establish a school primarily for Indians. An existing school in Connecticut, which happened to have as one of its trustees the Earl of Dartmouth, was moved by Wheelock to a site on the Connecticut River in the colony of New Hampshire, and in 1770 it opened its doors to four students as Dartmouth College. A board of American trustees was provided, but Wheelock remained as president until his death nine years later and was succeeded by his son. John Wheelock kept his job for 36 years, but he was unpopular and was caught up in the bitter politics between the Federalists and the Jeffersonian Republicans. In 1815 the trustees fired Wheelock.

The Jeffersonians made political hay of this action and used the issue to win power in the 1816 state elections. Their legislature then changed the private college into a state university and made John Wheelock its president. The two institutions used the same campus; the faculty and students split (most of them supporting the college); but there was only one seal and one set of records, and the courts had to decide who properly owned them. The question came before the Supreme Court dominated by the great Federalist John Marshall, with another anti-Jeffersonian, Dartmouth graduate Daniel Webster, pleading on behalf of the college. Marshall managed to transform the case into a historic affirmation of the sanctity of a charter as a contract, and the Court found for the college. The effect of the ruling was far-reaching because it severely limited the rights of the state legislatures. But with the fall of John Wheelock and the collapse of Dartmouth University, it was clear that the power of boards of trustees could not be challenged once it was established by state charter. The trustees had won some of this power from the faculty and the president in the colonial period, and had strengthened their position by including a number of state officials on their boards along with the dominant clerical members. Now Marshall's Court had secured them forever in formal command of higher education.

The decision also turned the tide in favor of the private, denominational type of college and indirectly against the state university. There was no hope of changing any private college already in operation into a state university. The private colleges were left to struggle for survival, dependent on the benefactions of friends and faith-fellows and whatever they could cajole from a state legislature. In the four decades between the Dartmouth College ruling and the Civil War, at least 800 college charters were granted. Only 145 of these institutions are still functioning. The United States countryside was littered with colleges, and the fittest did not always survive.

Is Education Necessary?

There was simply not enough money to support all the schools that were set up, many almost on impulse. This was not yet the age of great fortunes, and many of the benefactors were single-time donors, who offered a gift of modest sum and a library, sometimes as a bequest, or set aside lands to provide income. The Brown brothers of Providence, for instance, divided their energies between helping to found the College of Rhode Island and a variety of manufacturing and trading interests, including the provisioning of the Revolutionary Army. The son of one of them, Nicholas

Brown, a graduate of the college in 1786, learned of an offer in 1795 by the college president: "The corporation at their last meeting past a resolution that if a person would previous to the next Commencement, give to the College $6,000, he should have the right to name it." And this is how Brown University acquired its name.

Such incidents, although interesting, were not typical. The founding sect usually made the down payment, and solicited the rest through public subscriptions, promotions, lotteries, even "permanent scholarships" guaranteeing tuition in perpetuity to all the offspring of the contributing family. In many cases the state had to intervene with funds, and a question was raised as to how private an institution was when it solicited funds from the tax-supported revenues. Of course, the private colonial colleges had long accepted public funds, and had in turn welcomed public members to their boards of trustees. But this practice could hardly be extended to the hundreds of tiny sectarian institutions springing up helter-skelter.

The people who were expected to pay the bills, whether through donations or taxes, began to question the purpose and value of the institutions. Americans were busy, in these years, turning forests into farmlands, building roads and canals, surveying and exploring—the Louisiana Purchase alone was enough to tax the energies of a small nation. There was farming and trading and politicking and preaching to be done. Who needed a college education?

By candlelight in log cabins boys got what they could from books. The *principle* of general education was recognized in the Ordinance of 1785 for the Northwest Territory and in the constitutions of the states as they were carved out of that territory. But practice lagged behind principle. Except for higher education, there was no tradition, no framework, no experience. Somehow the people, especially with the rise of Jacksonian Democracy in the 1830's, developed a curious "love-hate" attitude toward the colleges. It was a mixture of scorn for teaching that appeared suitable only as a sort of ornamental veneer for "gentlemen" and of a fierce demand that whatever was good enough for the Founding Fathers must be made available, and fast, to all their posterity. Many were beginning to believe that higher education should be made useful and accessible. Others felt that as education became more "utilitarian" and was spread thinly and rapidly regardless of the capacity of those who were to receive it, the process would soon cease to be education in any real sense. The debate occupied the best minds in the field of education, and has not yet been decided.

Higher learning, handed down selectively from Cambridge in England to Cambridge in New England, was now to be passed on less selectively to Athens, Georgia, and Oxford, Ohio. For in the spirit of 19th-century democracy, which was extending the vote to all who were free, male, white, and over twenty-one, it was deemed fitting that this same segment of the population should be educationally processed for citizenship. First power, then knowledge.

Yale Stands Pat

The orthodox program was spelled out in a report prepared on order of the Yale Corporation and issued by President Jeremiah Day and his faculty in 1828. These teachers felt it to be their task to devote themselves to "the *discipline* and the *furniture* of the mind; expanding its powers, and storing it with knowledge." The customary technique for flexing the mental muscle (the "discipline" factor) was through the textbook, which was cited and re-cited (hence the sacred *recit*ation). From this point of view, class was a kind of setting-up exercise. As for the content to be stored, this too had been well established: "those subjects only which ought to be understood . . . by everyone who aims at a thorough education." Those who were properly programmed could later acquire any of the "furniture" (or accessories) that would equip them for practical living as lawyers, physicians, or politicians. As for other vocations, there was always the time-honored system of apprenticeship. "The young merchant must be trained in the counting room, the mechanic in the workshop, the farmer in the field." The new store of knowledge that was accumulating in the 19th century—the world of Eli Whitney, Robert Fulton, Cyrus McCormick, Samuel F. B. Morse, Samuel Colt—had no place on the New Haven campus. (Both Whitney and Morse were Yale graduates—but how much did they owe to its curriculum?)

The Yale Report of 1828 became a kind of model, setting the tone for the majority of early 19th-century colleges, old and new. It had an air of smug finality, such as one might expect from a corporation report (which it was): " . . . the changes in the country during the last century have not been greater than the changes in the college." A few teachers, such as George Ticknor of Harvard (who has broadened his outlook by studying at the reborn German universities) dissented: "The complaint is . . . that while every thing else is on the advance, our Colleges are stationary. . . . " The situation is well described by science historian Dirk Struik in *The Origins of American Science:*

While sailors plied the oceans to the Indias and to China, while self-made engineers built canals, bridges and turnpikes, and manufacturers, inventors and merchants laid the foundations of mass production, the colleges remained very quiet. Lecture halls and professorial chambers produced no great ideas and conceived no important projects.

But Jefferson Looks Ahead

Struik's conclusion is not quite fair. Some great ideas *were* produced, although few of them were implemented. The greatest, of course, was Thomas Jefferson's for the University of Virginia. For Jefferson was, as usual, abreast of his time —in fact, a little in advance of it—and did not hold with the Yale philosophy of education. As he saw it, there was a natural division in the population: some were destined to govern, others to labor. Each of these praiseworthy functions required proper training, and so far only the governors had received it. Now was the time to provide training for the governed as well.

The concept was relevant to the early years of the Industrial Revolution, with the first appearance of a sizable number of working people who could profit from such training. "Mechanics' institutions" had been set up in English cities to provide vocational skills for boys who would never go to such "public schools" as Eton and Harrow. (They were called "public" because pupils from outside the immediate community could attend them, but they were quite private and expensive.) Revolutionary France, which did little for elementary education, nevertheless was responsible for an École Polytechnique, set up in 1794. This school, which provided Napoleonic France—contemporary with Jeffersonian America—with great engineers, was an inspiration to Sylvanus

Thayer, who became superintendent of the recently established United States Military Academy in 1817. Under Thayer's guidance, according to Struik, "for several decades the engineering department [at West Point] had the field in America almost exclusively to itself."

The United States also saw the development of mechanics' institutes in the 1820's, but their functions were soon incorporated by the more progressive academies and colleges. Their image was preserved by Cooper Union, founded just before the Civil War in New York City, "to provide free courses of instruction in the application of Science and Art to the practical business of life." Except for West Point, the earliest institution of higher learning in the United States devoted primarily to practical training was set up at Troy, New York, in 1824 by the scion of a Dutch patroon family who was also a soldier, a politician, and a commissioner of the Erie Canal project. Stephen Van Rensselaer's School of Theoretical and Practical Science, was intended mainly to train instructors for "the sons and daughters of farmers and mechanics . . . in the application of experimental chemistry, philosophy, and natural history, to agriculture, domestic economy, the arts, and manufactures." Here were introduced the first field courses and the first laboratories for instruction, and in 1835 the Rensselaer Institute (as it was then called) produced eight graduates with the first American engineering degrees.

It was in this environment that Jefferson tried to open the college doors to the real world. Having failed to introduce reforms into his own alma mater, William and Mary, the former President devoted his last years to transforming the proposed new state university at Charlottesville into his ideal for such an institution. He proposed to jettison the classical pattern and replace it with a true university, comprising eight separate "schools," as follows: ancient languages, modern languages, mathematics, natural philosophy, natural history, anatomy and medicine, moral philosophy, and law. Students could choose among these schools and could choose courses within each school as their interests dictated. Each school would award a "diploma," but there was to be no degree.

This program was followed for seven years, then abandoned—possibly because the students were younger and less mature than anticipated. By 1831 the granting of a degree (M.A. rather than B.A.) was introduced, and the so-called elective system of choosing courses was modified. Educators in other colleges, however, took note of what was happening in Virginia and proved that Jefferson had not been wrong, but merely premature.

Applied Science Enters the Campus

In 1795 an academy at Schenectady, New York, had been chartered as Union College, and nine years later it was fortunate enough to secure as its president Eliphalet Nott, who held his post for the next 62 years. Being also an inventor (of the first anthracite-burning stove) and a good businessman, Nott amassed $600,000, which he gave to the college. He was also a courageous educator who succeeded in introducing a "modern" curriculum that de-emphasized Latin and Greek and allowed the substitution of such subjects as French, mathematics, and "science." Those who chose this "parallel" course were not awarded degrees, but Union became the fastest-growing college in the country, passing all others except Yale in registration in 1829. In 1845, perhaps influenced by the new trend at neighboring Rensselaer, Union also began to train civil engineers.

Yale itself finally experimented cautiously with "science." Curiously enough, it was the fear of science on the part of President Timothy Dwight, a strict Calvinist and zealous Federalist, that broke the ice. "Rather than turn his back upon natural science, he decided to have it taught by a man of reliable religious and political background," says Struik. The choice fell on twenty-three-year-old Benjamin Silliman, who had been appointed to teach chemistry and natural history at the college in 1802. Silliman became one of the great science popularizers in the country, but it was not until 1847 that he and his son were able to set up a special School of Applied Chemistry. Five years later a School of Engineering was founded at Yale, and in 1854 the two schools were merged as the Yale Scientific School. (When a benefactor was found, in the old tradition the name was changed to the Sheffield Scientific School.) Graduates were given a brand-new degree, Bachelor of Philosophy. Nevertheless, says Rudolph, students at the scientific school were "considered second-class citizens, too benighted to aspire to the only worthy degree . . . [They] were not permitted to sit with regular academic students in chapel."

By the middle of the 19th century the Massachusetts legislature was asking Harvard to undertake its share of the task of training "better farmers, mechanics, or merchants." It was such pressure, and perhaps the example of Yale, that stimulated Harvard to begin to slough off its classical skin. After all, the Lowell Institute had been providing a meeting place since 1839 for science-hungry Bostonians, and had

given a platform to some of the century's greatest scientists
—such men as Benjamin Silliman (who opened the Institute
lectures); botanist Asa Gray, a Harvard professor of natural
history since 1842; Charles Lyell, "father of geology," who
dedicated the account of his American travels to Harvard's
George Ticknor; and Louis Agassiz, Swiss naturalist, who
drew 1,500 people to his lectures at the Institute. Harvard,
aware of the action across the river, seized the opportunity
offered by a $50,000 gift from textile manufacturer Abbott
Lawrence, who asked:

> Where can we send those who intend to devote themselves
> to the practical application of science? How educate our
> engineers, our miners, machinists and mechanics? Our country
> abounds in men of action. Hard hands are ready to work
> upon our hard materials; and where shall sagacious heads be
> taught to direct those hands?

Why not at Harvard? Agassiz was persuaded to stay in the
United States as head of the new annex to Harvard, appropriately called the Lawrence Scientific School. Since Agassiz
was not an engineer, however, but one of the world's
greatest natural historians, the new school—whose graduates
were given an inferior B.S.—did not fill Lawrence's prescription, and it became necessary, after all, for the Massachusetts
legislature to charter a new polytechnic school modeled after
Rensselaer—the Massachusetts Institute of Technology.

Sluggish Colleges and Weak Academies

These, then, were the high spots in the reform of the
college curriculum before the Civil War in a half-hearted
effort to bring the institutions in line with society's requirements. There were other efforts, even less vigorous but more

directly affecting the rights and the composition of the student body. In the first category was that flash of insight on Jefferson's part—his proposal to allow students to choose for themselves. If this had been followed through, the sluggish change from classic to modern curriculum might have become torrential and altered the character of the United States college. In fact, this is what did happen after the Civil War. The delay of half a century can be attributed largely to the gap between those who ran the colleges and those who were concerned and involved with their actual operation—between the Overseers and the overseen faculty and students. For it was at this time, writes Walter P. Metzger in *Academic Freedom in the Age of the University,* that

> . . . a nadir seems to have been reached . . . the system of control by a nonresident board, carried over from the colonial colleges, evolved into an instrument of academic government that was officious, meddlesome, and often tyrannical. One finds the trustees of colleges prescribing the work of the classroom, writing the laws of student government, shaping the curriculum, subjecting the private lives of teachers to scrutiny and espionage.

The colleges of the first six decades of the 19th century did not attract vast numbers of young men. In the peak year of 1837, when there were about 100 degree-granting institutions, the student population was estimated at 10,000. (Compare the statistics of 1950, when the national population was ten times that of 1837: the nonveteran student population in college was about 1,600,000—*160 times* that of 1837.) However, since most of the colleges provided little more than the equivalent of a modern high school education, it would perhaps be fair to mention that in the mid-19th century a large number of private secondary schools were in operation—the academies—which did not grant degrees but provided education only slightly inferior to that of most of the colleges. Some 6,000 of these academies were operating in 1850, with more than 250,000 pupils. The academies, like the colleges, were devoted to the old "liberal" curriculum and were slow to introduce "modern" subjects such as mathematics, modern languages, and science. Like the colleges, they were essentially boarding schools and therefore served only that part of the population that could afford to send their teen-age sons away from home for an education.

The Minority Students Before the Civil War

Daughters had almost nowhere to go except to the female academies, which were sometimes known as seminaries. The best of these, such as Emma Willard's at Troy, New York, Catherine Beecher's Hartford Female Seminary, and Mary Lyon's Mount Holyoke Seminary, were comparable to the better colleges; and Mount Holyoke became a college in 1888. By that time there were more than a handful of colleges for women, the first of which opened in Macon, Georgia, in 1836. Wesleyan Female College, in 1840, was the first to confer a degree on a woman in the United States. The following year, three women graduated along with nine men from Oberlin, an experimental college chartered in Ohio in 1833.

Oberlin made history, not only because it was the first coeducational college in the country, but because it was the first to adopt a policy of admitting students "without respect to color." This policy drew to it the "radical" students of the day, although the college was by no means a hotbed of Abolitionism. A year after Oberlin was founded, it received an unexpected contingent from across the state. For at Lane Seminary in Cincinnati a crisis developed in 1834, described by a contemporary Oberlin student as follows:

> The Summer vacation of twelve weeks came on, and the Professors, with one exception, had left for the East. The students, too, were mainly scattered. The Trustees held a meeting at this juncture, and passed a law . . . prohibiting the discussion of slavery among the students, both in public and in private. . . . The students returned to enter their protest against the oppressive gag-law of the Trustees, and to ask dismissions from the institution. Four-fifths of them left in a body, and Lane Seminary has to this day never recovered from the blow.

The migrant students—who were surely unaware of the precedent set centuries earlier at Paris and Oxford—went to Oberlin in the spring of 1835. Lane Seminary disappeared, and Oberlin became a station on the Underground Railroad during the Civil War.

Oberlin was not the first college to accept a Negro student, however. That honor went to Amherst and Bowdoin, each of which graduated a Negro in 1826. There were also a few precursors of the "Negro colleges" that were to feature the Reconstruction South: the Ashmun Institute (later renamed Lincoln University), at Chester, Pennsylvania; Wilberforce, opened by the Methodists in western Ohio; and the Institute for Colored Youth (which became Cheyney College), opened near Philadelphia in 1837. But all such attempts were restricted to the North. In the Southern states it was generally a crime to teach a black person to read or write.

As shocking as this virtually complete neglect of the edu-

cation of young women and blacks may be, looking backward from our hardly exemplary late 20th century, it is
important to make judgments that relate to the entire society,
not merely to its educational aspect. For education always
has been, as it is today, a facet of the total society. And in
the first half of the 19th century there was no organized
demand, even on the part of these two oppressed minorities
(as we would term them now), for educational opportunities.
There was more demand than has been recognized for dignity
and freedom among the black population, and certainly here
and there the skill of reading and writing was sought and
won by individual blacks. A few whites in the North tried
to make a start in providing instruction on an organized
basis, as the existence of a handful of schools proves, but
there was no campaign to accomplish this.

It appears that girls, for the most part, accepted the role
assigned them by society, and when they sought "education," it was usually to fit them for that role. The sturdy
wives and daughters of west-bound settlers saw no need for
schooling. Their more effete sisters in towns and on planta-
tions back East were taught to be gracious and "accomplished." As a New England clergyman was told in 1782:

> We don't pretend to teach ye female part of ye town any-
> thing more than dancing, or a little music perhaps . . . ex-
> cept ye private schools for writing, which enable them to
> write a copy, sign their names &c, which they might not
> be able to do without such a privilege.

It was quite a leap from this to the classes in mathematics,
history, and physics in a small number of female seminaries
—but although the seminaries were available, there was no

surge of young women toward the campus until teaching became a profession after the Civil War.

Teachers and Students

The efforts to reform the curriculum and teaching methods failed to meet with general approval, even among the teachers. It was to be expected that a teaching profession, like other professions at later dates, would put up some resistance to innovations. But, as a matter of fact, there *was* no teaching profession. The colonial tutors, as we have observed, were mostly young and immature graduates who taught only until they could secure a ministerial post. Richard Hofstadter, in *Academic Freedom in the Age of the College,* reports:

> Harvard had been established for more than eighty-five years, Yale for more than fifty, and Princeton for more than twenty before each had its first professor, and it was to be many years before regular professors outnumbered transient tutors.

Throughout the entire period before the Civil War, most professors were clergymen, many of them unable and some of them unfitted to find a pastorate. Teaching was a thankless, ill-paid job and attracted few devoted or learned professionals. After all, the college was virtually a boarding school for adolescents, and the task of providing instruction was often less important than that of enforcing discipline. The students, free from parental control for the first time, bored with reciting texts, trapped in uncomfortable dormitories, poorly fed, and with few amusements, were an understandably raucous lot. According to John S. Brubacher and Willis Rudy, in *Higher Education in Transition:*

The hapless clergymen-professors of this era had to do more than teach; they were also required to be detectives, sheriffs, and prosecuting attorneys. In the case of general student disturbances, which under this system were endemic, the entire faculty would go on the chase for offenders!

In this era, the burden of the doctrine of *in loco parentis* was not on the dean, who had not been invented, but on the teacher. A president of Cornell University, Andrew Dickson White, recalled his school days:

> I had . . . known sundry college tutors seriously injured while thus doing police duty; I have seen a professor driven out of a room, through the panel of a door, with books, boots, and bootjacks hurled at his head; and even the respected president of a college, a doctor of divinity, while patrolling buildings with the janitors, subjected to outrageous indignity.

Such a faculty could hardly be expected to have enlightened views concerning the practice of their calling. Nor could they be expected to have much empathy for their "charges," who in turn regarded the teachers as their natural enemies. This chasm between the faculty and the students was fatal.

A student rebellion at Harvard in 1823 was the culmination of a series of "pranks" typical of the era, and a sign of the restlessness that could call forth only one reaction in those days: discipline. Morison tells of

> battles in commons, bonfires and explosions in the Yard, cannonballs dropped from upper windows, choruses of "scraping" that drowned tutors' voices in classroom and chapel, and plots that resulted in drenching their persons with buckets of ink-and-water.

It all ended, at least for the students, when 43 out of a class of 70 seniors were expelled. But for once the administration was worried, and two years later a new set of rules was drawn up. It included limited permission for the students to elect courses, but granting of this permission was left to the option of the heads of newly established departments, and only Ticknor's department accepted the option. Another innovation was a system of grading that turned out to be disastrous. According to Morison:

> This system poisoned the already hostile relations between students and instructors, and made social intercourse between them impossible. Almost every graduate of the period 1825–60 has left on record his detestation of the system of instruction at Harvard . . . the Faculty were not there to teach, but to see that boys got their lessons; to explain difficulties or elucidate a text would have seemed improper. [The students complained,] "No attempt was made to interest us in our studies."

At Amherst, an experimental course featuring history, English, modern languages, and the sciences was tried in 1826 but abandoned after two years, when it received no support from faculty, administration, or students. At Brown, President Francis Wayland threatened to resign in 1850 unless the Corporation adopted reforms he proposed, including an elective system under which "every student might study what he chose, all that he chose, and nothing but what he chose." After four years, falling enrollment forced abandonment of the plan, and in 1855 Wayland did resign. He was not unhappy, commenting: "No one can conceive the unspeakable relief and freedom which I feel at this moment to hear that bell rung, and to know, for the first time in nearly twenty-nine years, that it calls me to no duty."

This reaction is as understandable as the restlessness of the students and the insensitiveness of many of the teachers. For the president of a college or university was in the 19th century—and was to remain until the end of the century—a personage of great power and responsibility, if he chose to carry the load. He was already responsible to a board of trustees or regents, but such boards—although "meddlesome" if permitted—had not yet acquired the habit of massive intervention. The institutions were still manageable in size and able to respond to the personality of a president, as may be illustrated by three episodes occurring at the beginning, the middle, and the close of the period we are considering.

Harvard was under the presidency of a patriot-pastor, Samuel Langdon, during the Revolution. For some reason, he was unpopular with the students, who petitioned the Overseers to depose him. What is more remarkable, they wrote a letter to him, which closed with the following oft-quoted declamation that may or may not be a conscious imitation of Patrick Henry's cadence:

> As a man of genius and knowledge we respect you; as a man of piety and virtue we venerate you; as a President we despise you.

Langdon resigned.

The middle years were rife with student outbreaks, having no distinguishable pattern, and appearing on dozens of campuses. Morison gives this account of the most serious rebellion at Harvard in 1834:

> In the winter of that year the freshman and sophomore classes began to feel their oats. There were bonfires in the Yard, made more interesting by billets of wood secretly loaded with gunpowder. According to one account, the

Rebellion started from an altercation between a freshman and a callow young tutor in Greek; according to another, the freshmen and sophomores struck against . . . the Latin professor. . . . The Faculty, as usual, attempted to "make an example" of a few students; their classmates protested, at first by petition, and then, when that failed, by breaking the tutor's window, destroying his furniture, and ringing the college bell in the middle of the night. On May 29, 1834, all the sophomores were dismissed for the year, and ordered to leave town at once; and as soon as they had gone, the President announced that, since the college authorities were unable to discover those who had done the window-breaking damage (estimated at $300), the power of the Commonwealth would be invoked and the Grand Jury of Middlesex would root out the offenders and proceed against them by civil process.

Then hell broke loose! [President Josiah] Quincy had violated one of the oldest academic traditions: that the public authorities had no concern with what goes on inside a university so long as the rights of outsiders are not infringed. The "black flag of rebellion" was hung from the roof of Holsworthy [Hall]. Furniture and glass from the recitation rooms of University [Hall] were smashed, and the fragments hurled out of the windows. The juniors . . . voted to wear crape on their arms, issued a handbill with an acute dissection of the President's character, and hanged his effigy to the Rebellion Tree.

Finally, the students were sent one by one to the authorities at Concord to be examined, and "although two or three indictments were found, these were subsequently nol-prossed, and the whole business fizzled out. Quincy never regained his popularity."

Two years after this rebellion, Mark Hopkins became president of Williams College. A man of considerably less stature than Josiah Quincy, he nevertheless was able to establish an unusual rapport with his students. He was, in fact, the very model of the college professor, and he became famous in folklore because of James A. Garfield's comment, "The ideal college is Mark Hopkins on one end of a log and a student on the other." The epigram was delivered at an alumni gathering in 1871, three years after a crisis that occurred while President Hopkins was on a speaking trip. The Williams faculty at the time promulgated a rule tightening the requirements for attendance at recitations. Out of the 169 undergraduates, all but three signed a statement that they were prepared to leave the college rather than submit. They meanwhile struck classes and, after meeting with the faculty and winning no concessions, prepared to migrate as a body to the new Cornell University.

Then Hopkins came home, spoke with the students, and insisted that they acknowledge "the rightful authority of the faculty"; when most of them had done so, he saw to it that the rule was amended to the satisfaction of the students. End of ruckus.

Frederick Rudolph, who relates this story in his history of Williams, says in his preface that "few have understood how important to Mark Hopkins' college were the students at the other end of the log." At this period, not even the students understood.

CHAPTER FOUR

THE SHAPING OF
THE UNIVERSITY

EVEN BEFORE THE CIVIL WAR it was becoming obvious
that there was no future for an educational system that
propagated random colleges unrelated to social needs and
turned out a very small number of young gentlemen with
a classical background. But no one knew just what kind of
system should replace it.

Should the system be expanded in order to train a greater
number of such young gentlemen, thus lifting the general
educational level to that previously reserved for an elite? Or
should the system continue to produce an educated elite,
but one better equipped to cope with a society rapidly
changing under the influence of the Industrial Revolution?
As it turned out, neither formula would serve, and the great
debate was made academic by developments that were under
way even before the war ended.

The first development was that of a free, tax-supported
school system of "lower" education. Public elementary
schools were well established in a few Northeastern states
before the Civil War, but it was not until the 1860's that

they were extended rapidly from state to state until, except in the ravaged South, they had become customary.

Public secondary schools also began, in this era, to replace the academies of the boarding-school type, except for those few academies that promoted themselves into colleges. But the process was slow: As late as 1890, only 7 per cent of the children of high school age attended school. Many people doubted whether that much learning was needed for boys who were most likely to end up as farmers or mechanics, and they saw no reason to pay taxes to provide the colleges with expanding freshman classes. Just as the Dartmouth College case was a major factor in spreading private colleges throughout the country, so another court case seems to have turned the tide in favor of the public high school. This was a ruling of the Supreme Court of Michigan in 1874, which established the right of the citizens of Kalamazoo to support a secondary school just as the primary grades had been supported—from public taxes.

The practice spread through the country, and the number of high schools increased from just over 1,000 (with about 75,000 pupils) in 1870 to 6,000 (with more than 500,000 pupils) by the end of the century. As the high schools multiplied, there took form a unique educational feature, found only in the United States: the "ladder" extending without a break from kindergarten to postgraduate school.

The Minorities

Another development was education for females. At the elementary level, girls were mixed with boys from the start, and the practice was extended to the secondary schools so rapidly that as early as 1870 more girls than boys were in high schools—a situation that has continued to this day. Much of this trend may be ascribed to the recognition that women are ideally suited to teach the primary grades. Some of the better academies and seminaries had begun, before the Civil War, to prepare women teachers, who were recommended because they would do as well as men in this field for lower pay. A special kind of secondary school, called a "normal school" (from the French *école normale*), began to attract a strictly female student body. By 1890 there were more than 200 normal schools, but the regular secondary schools also graduated girls who could compete for teaching jobs in the primary grades. So the normal schools began to raise their sights and produce teachers for the secondary schools. In so doing, they assumed the right to grant a baccalaureate degree and called themselves "teachers colleges." It was not long before some of them became universities. And before the end of the century a number of colleges and universities, having embarked on the path of providing vocational training in so many fields, accepted teaching as a profession and offered degrees in education. Such a degree became virtually a requirement for a career teacher beyond the primary grades.

After the Civil War, even girls who did not intend to teach began going to college. A few degree-granting colleges for females already existed, but none offered an education beyond the secondary level. When established colleges such as Oberlin became coeducational and when newly founded institutions adopted coeducation as a policy, as did Antioch and many Western state universities, the groundwork was laid. But it was not until Vassar Female College opened in

1861, endowed by a generous brewer, that education of the quality found in the better men's colleges became available to women who preferred "separate but equal" status. Soon Smith and Wellesley were founded for the same purpose, but by that time (1875) women were first-class citizens at Cornell University and at state universities from Michigan to California. In the end, the coeducational principle was to prevail—even at Vassar. By 1880, women were studying at half the institutions of higher learning; by 1900 at seven out of ten. Indeed, according to Christopher Jencks and David Riesman, girls accounted for most of the increased enrollment in the comeback of the colleges just after the Civil War.

The black minority fared poorly on the college scene. The "emancipated" black, like his brother in the Congo a century later, was abruptly placed by his oppressors in the impossible position of finding a place in society for which he had not been prepared. Denied—in fact, forbidden—a rudimentary education, he was thrust out of slavery without even the "forty acres and a mule" that he had been led to expect. For one of the obligations of the Bureau of Refugees, Freedmen and Abandoned Lands (known in history courses as the Freedmen's Bureau, and set up in the War Department in 1865) was to assign 40-acre plots—an agrarian reform that never did get under way. Another was to set up free schools, which it did, apparently with the enthusiastic support of the chief commissioner, General Oliver Otis Howard.

After the reconstructed whites had suffocated the elementary schools, all that remained of the Freedmen's Bureau effort were the university named after General Howard and a number of other so-called colleges. The most effective of these were Fisk University at Nashville, also named for a general, and Hampton Institute, at Hampton, Virginia, both founded with the help of the American Missionary Association (an agency of the Congregational Church).

From these two institutions developed diverging notions of the higher education of blacks. Fisk hewed to the traditional "liberal" education, which many attacked as unsuitable for semiliterate former slaves. But those who defended the concept believed that if this kind of education was good for whites, it must also be good for blacks. (Unfortunately, it was not always good for either.) Hampton, on the other hand, started out as an agricultural and normal school, was properly named a land-grant college by Virginia (more about this later), and produced as a graduate Booker T. Washington. It was Washington's fate to incarnate what most blacks today consider an "Uncle Tom" concept of black education, which he had applied as the first head of Tuskegee Normal and Industrial Institute in Alabama.

For the decades after their founding Hampton and Tuskegee and the scores of small Negro "colleges" that were set up by church groups did a job that white society was not going to do. They gave minimal skills to students who were lifting themselves by their bootstraps to a secondary school level, and they produced a generation of ministers and teachers who would continue the process, laying a foundation for a day when actual college education could be placed on the agenda. By 1900, after some 200 Negro colleges had been founded and half of them had perished, those that survived had to accept the help of Northern whites to sustain a network of Negro institutions.

Federal Blessing for Vocationalism

It was no accident that the training provided for the relatively large number of newly enrolled girl and black students, after the Civil War, was largely vocational. The trend toward "practical" training had appeared long before the war, and was gathering momentum. It had been reflected in the introduction of scientific and practical courses in some of the colleges, in the establishment of a few institutions oriented essentially toward technology, and in attempts to organize a curriculum around such subjects as agricultural chemistry and experimental research.

As early as 1838 an American who had studied at the Royal Agricultural School in Bavaria pointed out to Congress the advances that were being made in Europe in scientific farming, advances that could and should be applied to the task of cultivating most of a continent. The Michigan constitution of 1850 had provided for a school of agriculture, and in 1857 Michigan State College of Agriculture had been founded at East Lansing. Two years earlier, Pennsylvania had chartered the Farmers High School, which by 1861 was awarding its graduates the degree of Bachelor of Scientific Agriculture. (Eventually these institutions were to become Michigan State and Pennsylvania State universities.) The stage was set for one of the landmark happenings in United States educational history: the passage of the Morrill Act of 1862, which established the system of land-grant colleges.

Justin Smith Morrill, a Vermont farmer beginning a 44-year tenure in the U.S. Congress, had introduced in 1857 a bill to support institutions that would "teach such branches of learning as are related to agriculture and the mechanic arts"; Congress had accepted the measure, but President Buchanan vetoed it. In 1862, a year of spectacular legislation, President Lincoln signed the Morrill Act. It provided the several states with the income from the sale of about 10,000,000 acres of Federal land, to be used for

> the endowment, support, and maintenance of at least one college [in each state] where the leading object shall be . . . to teach such branches of learning as are related to agriculture and the mechanic arts . . . in order to promote the liberal and practical education of the industrial classes in the several pursuits and professions in life.

Except for the general land grants of the Northwest Ordinance of 1785 (which had resulted in establishment of some state universities) and the founding of the United States Military Academy in 1802, this was the first sign that the Federal government was concerned with higher education. The military academy had been established because no institution was then in existence capable of providing trained personnel for the armed forces. Apparently the government took the view that there were still not enough institutions in existence capable of training personnel for the farms, mines, and factories of the growing nation.

The people of the United States were engaged in bringing food and metals out of the enormous estate they had acquired. They were planting towns along the railroad rights-of-way and beginning to use the equipment that was becoming available at a bewildering rate—from nail machines and barbed wire to the rotary press, the Bessemer converter, and all manner of farm equipment—and no amount of Latin or moral philosophy was likely to prove helpful in solving the problems they faced. The Morrill Act was an effective answer to the elitist traditionalism of the Yale Report of 1828. It also helped restore the balance that had been upset by the Dartmouth College decision, for it favored the state universities as against the private colleges—although many of the latter were designated beneficiaries of the land-grant provisions by state legislatures.

One would think that a society still 85 per cent rural would welcome the new direction, but critics outnumbered enthusiasts. Even academic innovators such as President Charles W. Eliot of Harvard looked down their noses at the "cow colleges," and there were snorts from the farm spokesmen:

> Instead of introducing the student of agriculture to a laboratory and chemical and philosophical apparatus, we would introduce him to a pair of heavy neat's leather boots and corduroy pants, and learn him to load manure.

There was no rush to the new agricultural and mechanical (soon shortened to "A & M") institutions or to the older colleges that received land-grant status; even Justin Morrill's own state of Vermont had no student of agriculture at its university ten years after the act was passed. Nevertheless, the states duly distributed the funds from the land sales—which proved to be less than expected—to their state universities, to existing agricultural schools (as in Michigan and Pennsylvania), to new institutions that were or included A & M institutes, or to private colleges. Among the beneficiaries were the Sheffield Scientific School at Yale; Massachusetts Institute of Technology; Dartmouth College; Brown University; and in New Jersey, Rutgers Scientific School, to which the president of Princeton snidely referred as an "excellent college at New Brunswick, managed by a few Dutchmen." An entirely new phenomenon was Cornell University, which combined the private endowment of a telegraph tycoon with the New York State College of Agriculture to take over the state's land-grant benefits in a burst of glory. An instant college, it opened in 1867 with a freshman class of 412 men and women—seven years after Harvard had achieved its first senior class of 100.

Electives and the Graduate School

Harvard's Eliot defended his college against the assault of what he considered rank vocationalism:

> The whole tone and spirit of a good college ought to be different in kind from that of a good polytechnic or scientific school. In the college, the desire for the broadest culture, for the best formation and information of the mind, the enthusiastic study of subjects for the love of them without any ulterior objects, the love of learning and research for their own sake, should be dominant ideas. . . . The student in a polytechnic school has a practical end constantly in view.

Eliot practiced what he preached, and despite his flair for elitism, his administration provided one of the major breakthroughs that led to the modern university. When he went to Harvard from MIT (a "good polytechnic or scientific school," to be sure), where he had taught chemistry, he became the first nonclerical president in Harvard's history. By this time, according to Morison, "nothing had been done to solve the great question of modernizing the undergraduate curriculum; nobody had yet found any acceptable compromise between the literary and classical subjects which everyone admitted were good, and the natural and social sciences which most people believed to merit more recognition." Eliot changed all this, not in order to equip Harvard graduates with technological know-how, but because he believed a course in physics, properly taught, could yield as much cultural value as a course in moral philosophy. In the sixth year of his forty-year administration he virtually ended the ancient rigidity of the curriculum and allowed all except freshmen to choose most of their study programs. Nine years later freshmen were given the same privilege.

The major colleges and the small citadels of the liberal arts fought back, but Eliot had opened a Pandora's box—and although the results may have dismayed him, he never wavered, and his reforms stuck and spread. For the 19th century had spawned more knowledge and more branches of knowledge than any period before, and the United States was eager to absorb whatever was offered—as the popularity of the lecture circuits and the Chautauqua movement proved. Now the colleges began to offer courses in architecture, public health, economics, history, palaeontology, geography, English literature—a thousand flowers, with no coercion and no guidance. The abundance of subject matter forced the organization of departments, and where formerly there had been "natural philosophy," now there were biology and chemistry and geology and other sciences, each with a measure of autonomy. Soon biology became zoology and botany, and various sub-branches began to emerge. The Yale catalogue could no longer print its curriculum on one page, as it had done in 1829.

The rich diversity of subjects reflected, not merely curiosity and an awakening sense of the expansion of knowledge, but an urgent desire to appropriate the knowledge for practical ends—whether or not this pleased the Eliots. Many of the new land-grant colleges, especially Cornell and the large state universities, expanded their curricula at a rate exceeding that of most of the established institutions, and they did so under the stimulus of providing the vocational services for which they were established. Since they also continued to provide a "liberal" course for those who desired it, whereas a tinge of vocationalism began to appear at Harvard, Columbia, and eventually even at Yale, the differences between these institutions tended to diminish. At the same time, a great gulf separated all of them from the staid "pure" liberal arts colleges that continued in the venerable tradition. There began to appear, in short, a group of universities and a group of colleges. Although the former group still lacked essentials to true university rank, this lack was repaired before the 19th century had come to a close.

The medieval university had developed a number of faculties, beyond that of arts, which granted advanced degrees certifying that graduates could practice such professions as medicine, law, or theology. At Oxford and Cambridge, it became customary for the master's degree to be conferred on a bachelor for a fee and without additional study after a given number of years—"in course," as the phrase was. This procedure was inherited by United States colleges, and Harvard continued to give a master's "in course" until 1872.

Professional education in England owed little to the universities—training for the law, for example, was taken out of their hands and assigned to the Inns of Court in the 13th century. On the continent of Europe and in Scotland, however, the doctorate (which was generally preferred over the master's) continued to signify professional competence; the first American M.D. came from the University of Göttingen in 1787. The German universities that were restored or established after the Napoleonic period—at Berlin, Bonn, Göttingen—began to attract scholars from the United States, beginning with George Ticknor and three others in 1815; at least 200 Americans studied at these universities before the Civil War.

They returned home with reports of a new kind of education, which stressed a devotion to scholarship and a freedom to learn and teach that were unknown elsewhere. Both students and teachers were considered responsible members of a community of scholars, and they were allowed to pursue their search for knowledge without interference from any source. The concept of academic freedom was derived from the practices followed in the German universities of that time. There Ticknor observed the elective system and other related freedoms granted to students, so different from the boarding-school environment prevailing at colleges in the United States. He saw and reported the respect accorded to teachers, who were encouraged to add to their store of knowledge without neglecting their teaching duties. Students attended lectures, observed laboratory experiments, sometimes participated in research with their instructors in seminars. The professions were staffed with graduates, and the degree of Doctor of Philosophy was a high honor as well as a certificate of proficiency, for it had been earned.

These reports began to have an impact in the United States even before the Civil War, and Jefferson had been especially attracted by the elective principle. When the

University of Virginia began to offer a degree, it was the master's. Henry Tappan, who tried and failed to introduce some of the German features at the University of Michigan, nevertheless persuaded the regents for a few years to offer the M.A. and M.S. degrees. Columbia also toyed with the idea. In 1861, Yale granted the first American Ph.D. degrees to three students graduating from its advanced schools of philosophy and psychology, physics, and the classics.

The graduate school leading to an advanced degree was an entirely separate development from the professional school, which might lead to a bachelor's or to no degree at all. In the United States, before the Civil War, physicians and lawyers were generally trained through an apprenticeship system—on-the-job office work, and no questions asked when the shingle was displayed. But there were a few famous training centers outside the colleges, such as Tapping Reeve's Litchfield Law School in Connecticut, the Philadelphia College of Pharmacy, the Baltimore College of Dental Surgeons, and a number of medical schools. Courses in medicine and law were also offered at several of the larger colleges. The new profession of engineering was first staffed from special institutions such as the U.S. Military Academy and Rensselaer, then by the scientific schools set up by Yale and Harvard just before the Civil War. But all of these courses were undergraduate, except those at Yale. Harvard established its first graduate Department of Arts and Sciences leading to an advanced degree in 1872—the year the last "in course" degree was granted.

Debut of the American University

In 1873 a millionaire merchant named Johns Hopkins died in Baltimore and left a large part of his estate to a board of trustees who were directed to proceed with the establishment of a new kind of university. They selected as its first president a Yale graduate, Daniel Coit Gilman, who had taught at the Yale Scientific School and had become president of the new University of California. An apostle of the German educational theory, Gilman proceeded to set up graduate faculties—and *only* graduate faculties—on the German model at Johns Hopkins University. He began with a school of philosophy, then arts and sciences, and in 1893 the school of medicine, for which the institution became especially noted, largely because it was associated with a well-equipped hospital (another Johns Hopkins bequest).

Professors of the greatest eminence were invited to join these faculties, and were promised facilities for research, also in the German tradition, and unavailable at any other school in the United States. Out of 150 applicants, 21 choice students—"men of mark," Gilman rightly called them —were attracted by fellowships, and the German techniques of lecture, laboratory, and seminar were exclusively employed; all courses were elective. The success of the program, in terms of stated aims, is proved by the finding, 50 years after its founding, that one-fourth of the nation's 1,000 top scientists had received their training at Johns Hopkins.

As if the educators of the country had been awaiting a cue, they began to fall into line. Outright imitators were few—there were not many administrators of the stature of Gilman, nor were there enough first-rate professors or, for that matter, first-rate students to go around. G. Stanley Hall, after teaching psychology at Johns Hopkins for eight years, tried to export the graduate university idea to Massachusetts in the very year (1889) that Johns Hopkins itself found it expedient to develop a supporting undergraduate division. But Hall's sponsor, Jonas Gilman Clark, withdrew his approval after three years; Clark University, at Worcester, Massachusetts, also reverted to the conventional pattern, and a large part of its faculty moved on to the newly established University of Chicago.

In Chicago the Rockefeller millions and the genius of William Rainey Harper were about to exploit the Hopkins formula with variations. The chief variation was an enrollment, before the doors opened, of almost 600 students and a faculty of 120, the latter acquired by raiding other institutions; nine former college presidents were in the catch. Chicago had both a graduate and an undergraduate division from the start, with suitable distinctions in techniques. The "major and minor" system was created for the most advanced section, and the annual "class" system was obliterated. Grinds could study in all four of the quarterly terms (instead of the normal three) and so rush pell-mell toward Commencement.

The impact of Johns Hopkins and the University of Chicago on the established colleges was sufficient to turn many of them into universities, too. Harvard, which was well on its way toward achieving its own laurels under Eliot, had begun to award earned M.A. and Ph.D. degrees, the latter requiring a dissertation considered to be "a contribution to knowledge." (At Hopkins, the thesis had to be printed.) A Harvard Ph.D. in mathematics was granted in 1873. Eliot affirmed, at the 25th anniversary of Johns Hopkins, that his host university's example had "forced our Faculty to put their strength into the development of our instruction for graduates. And what was true of Harvard was true of every other university in the land which aspired to create an advanced school of arts and sciences."

Columbia College set up a graduate faculty of political science in 1880, and it added two others—philosophy and pure science—before 1896, when it first began to call itself a university. Princeton University emerged that same year, having until then flourished under the name of the College of New Jersey, but its graduate school was not in operation until 1900. Yale had long since joined the club, winning legislative approval of its new status in 1887. As for the state universities, they had long used the name without deserving it, so they now proceeded to play the game by acquiring graduate faculties. But many of them, including the largest, were wedded to the land-grant obligations of vocational training. They began, successfully, to light the torch at both ends, producing bachelors who knew their fertilizers and an increasing quota of masters and doctors impregnated with higher learning. As Rudolph comments:

> At Ithaca it seemed as though a university was being defined as a place where anything could be studied, as a place where physical chemistry, Greek, bridge-building, the diseases of the cow, and military drill, were equal.

Well, hadn't Ezra Cornell declared: "I would found an institution where any person can find instruction in any study"?

Advancement of Learning

One further item remained to complete the bequest of the German university to higher education in the United States. This item was the primacy of research, and it was the core of the system. German boys were selected to attend the *Gymnasium*—the college-preparatory school—because they had the makings of scholars; they were dedicated to scholarship. At the university, they were in a sense preparing for a life in the service of learning, and they were expected, when they received their doctorates, not merely to preserve and hand down to another generation their inherited store of knowledge, but to add to the store. The elective principle in studying, the teaching techniques, the contents of the curriculum, the fantastic attention to detail that turned the footnote into a kind of literary genre—all these enormously impressed foreigners. But there was no point in selecting one or another aspect in isolation, for it was the combination that counted. The *Gymnasium* and the university were organized and structured to lead to the advancement of learning, in a sense not contemplated by Francis Bacon. Rudolph cities Daniel C. Gilman, writing in *The Building of the University:* "The university is the most comprehensive term that can be employed to indicate a foundation for the promotion and diffusion of knowledge—a group of agencies organized to advance the arts and sciences of every sort, and train young men as scholars for all the intellectual callings of life."

The old questions—whether to educate an elite, how much of an elite to educate, how to educate them—were less relevant in this context. Here the emphasis was not on education in the old liberal arts sense of producing good citizens and leaders of men; nor on training in the vocational sense of equipping prospective farmers, miners, factory managers, schoolteachers, even enginers or ministers, to do a job. It was rather a kind of dedication: production of scholars who would in turn produce more scholars, thus advancing knowledge for the benefit of the human race. "The promotion and diffusion of knowledge" became virtually a cult, established for the king of Prussia by Wilhelm von Humboldt, friend of Goethe and Schiller, a foremost liberal of his day. Humboldt had stated it unequivocally:

> The State should not look to the universities for anything that directly concerns its own interests, but should rather cherish a conviction that in fulfilling their real function, they will not only serve its purposes but serve them on an infinitely higher plane . . . affording room to set in motion much more efficient springs and forces than are at the disposal of the State itself.

Or, in modern translation, give education as an idea a chance and it will pay off in practice. Humboldt's system, which also comprised polytechnic institutes after the French model, was largely responsible for German leadership in certain aspects of 19th-century culture, from a monopoly in philology to a very profitable lead in chemistry. It was Humboldt's brother, Alexander, who got Justus von Liebig his job at Giessen, and it was Liebig who developed the first research laboratory for students in Europe—and also made organic chemistry an independent science. Such laboratories spread outward from Germany and across the Atlantic, making it necessary for every self-respecting university to build one or more science laboratories to go with their hitherto neglected libraries and rising stadiums.

It was only appropriate that the laboratory in which atomic fission first proved successful (in 1942) should be at the University of Chicago, for President Harper had set a fateful course for American higher education 50 years earlier by proclaiming: "It is proposed in this institution to make the work of investigation primary, the work of giving instruction secondary." This dynamic not only would lead ultimately to the Manhattan Project but also would scatter some of the elementary particles of American education in unforeseen directions.

The new university proved as successful as sex. It introduced the reproductive principle, each generation producing through its graduate schools a quota of new participants in the system (one could not always term them "teachers") and at the same time generating a further fragmentation and accretion of knowledge, yielding more grist for the curriculum. The information explosion was well under way once research had begun to take over.

The differences between the German and American environments accounted for the divergent development of the university in the two cultures. In Germany the students moving from *Gymnasium* to university were well prepared, relatively mature (about twenty years of age), with similar middle-class backgrounds and similar motivations to occupy an intellectual niche. University graduates, whether they had become philologists or mathematicians, physiologists or physicists, belonged to a single scholarly community with a unique position in society.

The scene in the United States was quite different. The full-fledged university developed while the country was expanding, finding itself, and also absorbing the full impact of the Industrial Revolution. The educational system below college level was being formed very tentatively. It was not until the end of the 19th century that public high school enrollment doubled that of the colleges. By that time the high schools had displaced the academies and were beginning to displace some of the smaller colleges as well, because the latter charged tuition and often required residence for an education that was not far above secondary school level. Most boys and girls did not proceed from high school to college because, unlike the *Gymnasien,* the high schools were not set up primarily for college preparation. Moreover, most parents considered that high school itself was a tremendous educational advance compared to what had been available to them, and saw no reason for pushing their children still another step forward. In 1900, about 9 per cent of the high school age group were enrolled in schools, while only 4 per cent of the eighteen to twenty-one age group were on college rolls. The high schools continued to grow at a faster rate than the colleges until, by the 1940's, about 65 per cent of the eligible children were attending either public or private high schools, while about 15 per cent of college-age youth sought further education.

Success Story

Clearly no rush to the campus ensued—and this despite the encouragement given by the Morrill Act. It had been necessary to pass a second Morrill Act in 1890, for the funds from the land grants were about exhausted, and the "industrial classes" in the South were dealt out of the educational game by the intransigent rebels who ran 17 of the states.

One provision of the new legislation took care of the financial problem by assigning annual grants to the states to maintain and extend the A & M network, and another forced the Southern states to bring the black population into the fold, although—in the spirit of the times—the legislation provided that separate but equal institutions would meet the requirements of the Federal government. Most of the land-grant colleges in the South were less than second-rate to begin with, but those set up after 1890 were not even good high schools and received no local support. Historian Charles Beard, a liberal, reported that the program for the blacks was not so bad: "According to the best estimates, forty years after emancipation, at least one-half of the Negroes in the United States were reported as able to read or write." He failed to stress the fact that one-half could not.

Bigots could be expected to oppose the expansion of education, and many who opposed it on other grounds turned bigot—some even labeled the land-grant program "socialistic." Of course, the less secure private colleges wanted to discourage the competition. Intended beneficiaries of the Morrill legislation, the organized farmers of the Grange, at first considered the schooling of farmers a waste of tax money, especially since so much of the schooling was the classical routine of the effete East, but when the A & M institutions offered courses their sons could understand, rural opposition tended to wane. The Hatch Act of 1887, which set up experiment stations that could act as laboratories for the practical courses in the colleges, was a great booster. The clincher was the "Wisconsin idea," which made the state universities virtual community centers at which farmers, businessmen, and entrepreneurs could seek advice and even take extension courses to solve their day-to-day problems. The notion of the college as a service institution was quite new, and it proved popular, whereas the snob appeal of a college education had repelled. Wisconsin was so enamored of the concept that before World War I the state was largely staffed by University of Wisconsin trainees and faculty.

Another sign of the increasing popularity of the state university was its enrollment rate, which was not spectacular but was 50 per cent higher than that of the private universities in the East. Part of this growth had a financial basis; to residents of the state, the tuition was free or minimal and the campus was accessible. The practical courses appealed to legislators. The competition—not only the crossroads colleges that still struggled for survival, but the great institutions with their impressive faculties and "name" value— had to buy bricks, books, and brains without benefit of tax money. A few still had benefit of clergy—the denominational college continued to operate—but the mood toward the end of the 19th century was increasingly secular, and the churches were no longer pouring as much money into education as they were devoting to missionary work. On the other hand, the industrial wheels were turning; the robber barons were busy developing their fiefs; the railroads and telegraph lines had returned enough wealth to endow their owners with a sense of generosity. So the fortunes piled up, and the Foundation was born—a 19th-century version of the benefactions that had named so many institutions.

Some of the old-style largesse was still left. Ezra Cornell, Cornelius Vanderbilt, Johns Hopkins come to mind, but the multimillions came from a California railroad tycoon, Leland Stanford, and an unschooled dynasty founder, John Davison Rockefeller. The Stanford experience, despite the lavish spending, revealed the most shameful features of the paternalism—in this case, maternalism—that private benefaction can impose. The donor's widow humiliated President David Starr Jordan of Stanford University for more than a decade, but he outlived her and made "her" university (as she literally considered it) a respectable center of research. Rockefeller, on the other hand, poured money into the University of Chicago and allowed the experts to run the show. He also allotted vast sums to other aspects of education—especially medical research and the improvement of facilities for the educationally deprived. A number of wealthy Northerners, in fact, attempted with middling success to take over the role that the Southern Establishment had rejected.

The first educational foundation, established by financier George Peabody, became virtually an endowment for a single institution, the then decrepit University of Nashville. This institution exemplified the frustrations of the early-19th-century college. Founded as Davidson Academy in 1785, it became Cumberland College in 1806 and 20 years later called itself the University of Nashville. In 1824 it acquired as president a brilliant and ambitious educator, Philip Lindsley, who offered the frontier population more than they were ready to accept in the way of liberal education. Other colleges sprang up in the area until by 1848 they numbered 30, nine of them within 50 miles of Nashville, and Lindsley's university was unable to withstand the competition. In 1875 Peabody came to the rescue, however, and the institution was downgraded to a normal school and took its benefactor's name. The public education of Southern whites was greatly indebted to the supply of teachers from Peabody. With the dissolution of the fund in 1914, the bulk of the remaining money went to the George Peabody College for Teachers; the remaining $350,000—out of a total expenditure of about $2,600,000—went to Negro education by way of the previously established Slater fund.

New England textile manufacturer John F. Slater in 1872

had set aside $1,000,000 "for the uplifting of the lately emancipated people of the Southern States," and this money went to train teachers for the segregated blacks. As the years went by, other funds (including the residue of the Peabody) were added. With allocation of additional Rockefeller millions in 1902 to form the General Education Board, the Jim Crow educational system in the South was firmly funded. This made it possible for the grudging taxpayers of the region to provide as little as 37 per cent of the total cost of educating blacks as late as 1930.

The other educational benefactions by Rockefeller before World War I and by Andrew Carnegie as well were in the old tradition—the establishment of named memorials: the Rockefeller Institute (now Rockefeller University) and the Carnegie Institute. Carnegie, however, also provided $15,000,000 in a foundation "for the advancement of teaching," which had an impact on education not spelled out in the terms of the gift. The donor provided pensions for teachers in higher education, but in doing so, specified the kinds of institutions whose employees could benefit from the largesse. The Carnegie Foundation in effect drew a line between "good guys" and "bad guys" among all the practicing colleges, universities, and technical institutions in the United States—a task not attempted by any governmental authority. The approved institutions could therefore attract teachers without necessarily offering top salaries, because of the accruing pension privileges. The disapproved institutions could either change their ways or suffer from the competition. Many changed their ways—by converting to nonsectarianism, for example, or by hiring more Ph.D.'s, but never by desegregation. In fact, as it turned out, the Carnegie Foundation became the official but very powerful arbiter of what was and what was not acceptable in higher education. On the whole, educators felt, it was about time some authority was able to separate the wheat from the chaff. When the Foundation extended its dominion to the area of college entrance, it gave its name to the familiar Carnegie unit, which made bookkeeping easier for admissions officers.

Another source of funds for higher education before World War I was the organized graduates. An early instance of alumni interest was the recommendation of the Harvard Alumni Association, at its tenth anniversary in 1852, to endow an annual scholarship. The formation of alumni associations had a triple thrust. Such associations provided sources of contributions for the institutions, as expanding plant and faculty outstripped their customary resources. The children of alumni were natural candidates for enrollment. Most important of all, the alumni took an interest—sometimes a commanding interest—in the policies of their alma maters. As President Noah Porter of Yale said in 1870: "Alumni . . . retain and somewhat liberally exercise the traditional privileges of all children, freely to criticise the ways of the household."

The New Apparatus

What better way of criticizing than from the inside? Clerical monopoly of the governing boards had begun to give way in the 18th century with the addition of state officials (as at Yale). Insofar as the state helped to fund the institutions—even the private colleges—this seemed fair. For the same reason, as the 19th century progressed, businessmen had begun to occupy trustee seats hitherto held by the clergy. In 1851 the Harvard charter was amended to make this possible, providing that most of the Overseers should be elected by the legislature regardless of whether or not they were clergymen. In 1865 the elections were turned over to each year's graduates on Commencement Day; and by 1916 all Harvard graduates could vote for their Overseers. The trend in most colleges was to choose "sound" citizens; if they also had fortunes, so much the better. Alumni donations and alumni bequests became a staple without which, before long, no institution of higher learning could survive. College administrators appealed "to the leaders of business enterprise for endowments, they drafted men of money into the service of collegiate direction," wrote Charles and Mary Beard, "until at the end of the [19th] century the roster of American trustees of higher learning read like a corporation directory."

Trustees of this type were not expected to participate in the day-to-day activities of the institutions they held in trust. Yet the administration of the university, with its growing physical estate, higher enrollment, larger faculties, and more complex structure, had outgrown the paternal supervision of a president, even one with the capacity of an Eliot, a Gilman, or a Harper. The second half of the 19th century therefore saw further developments: the growth of an administrative apparatus in support of the front office; and a new relationship between the faculty and the administration. The full hierarchy of the modern university began to take shape.

Even after the Civil War, it was not unusual for a university president to remain an active educator. Michigan's

James Angell not only taught classes, but also acted as registrar; and Timothy Dwight, Yale's second president of that name, who took office in 1886, was the first non-teaching head of that university, although he had previously taught at the divinity school for almost 30 years. At about the same time, Harvard's Eliot, who advised Gilman of Johns Hopkins not to overwork himself, took over the administrative leadership with his usual thoroughness, sitting on every committee and board as the departmental mechanism began its inexorable growth. He appointed the first dean of the college in 1870. Dean Gurney was also a teaching professor but, according to Brubacher and Rudy, his main nonteaching task was

> . . . to take the burden of discipline off President Eliot's shoulders. In 1890, a Board of Freshman Advisers was set up at Harvard and the deanship was divided into two offices. . . . This pattern tended to become general in Middle Western and Western universities in the early twentieth century; soon it was established in Eastern institutions as well. Everywhere two types of deans made their appearance: "academic deans" of colleges or special faculties (who were primarily educational administrators) and "deans of students" . . . . whose concern was with the extracurricular life of undergraduates. Then, as enrollments continued to mount, various forms of specialized counseling began to branch off from the latter office. The sheer physical burden of handling student problems was becoming too great for one man, especially in the larger universities. By the time of the First World War the administrative staffs dealing with these problems began to proliferate and diversify. Directors of admission now came to be appointed, and placement and health officers too.

What had happened to Mark Hopkins' log? A forest of

personnel sprang up, some of it to provide protective shade
to the students, but along with it a wilderness of func-
tionaries more appropriate to a business organization than
to an institution of higher learning. Rudolph offers a graphic
description of the situation as of 1914:

> On one assembly line the academicians, the scholars, were
> at work: from time to time they left *their* assembly line
> long enough to oil and grease the student assembly line.
> . . . Above them, around them were the managers—the
> white-collared, chief executive officers and their assistants.
> The absentee stockholders, sometimes called alumni; the
> board of directors, at some places called the trustees or
> overseers; the untapped capital resources, known as bene-
> factors and philanthropic foundations; the regulatory
> agencies and the commissions in charge of standards—by
> the First World War they were, on one level, what was
> meant by higher education in the United States.

These developments, which had turned the president into
a chief executive, necessarily altered the character of the
faculty. The warden's role had long since been taken over
by the dean or by one of the student government bodies that
began to appear. Relations with students were also improved
as an indirect result of the elective system, for it freed both
teachers and students from a stifling rigidity and made
them partners in the pursuit of knowledge—an original purpose of the university. In the second half of the 19th century,
college teaching had become a profession.

One sign of professionalism appeared to be an indifference to material reward. Concern about wages was un-
dignified and unworthy; Rudolph cites editorial comment
from *The New York Times, The Nation,* and the *New Republic*
showing that professors were expected to disdain money as

early as 1883 and as late as 1930, and in the middle of this span stands President Eliot's rather smug observation: "The profession can never be properly recruited by holding out pecuniary inducements."

Another evidence of the new status was the appearance of rank in the faculties, attaining an early absurdity at the University of Chicago when President Harper appointed almost a dozen grades to provide a sense of "upward mobility" in place of the compensation available to other employees.

The schedule of the teacher's progress in 1891 was as follows: fellow, reader, lecturer, docent, assistant, associate, instructor, assistant professor, associate professor, professor, and head professor. In that same year about 150 Ph.D.'s were granted throughout the country. It was not long before the Ph.D. was required for the higher grades of the "professoriat." When only colleges with six full professors were declared eligible for Carnegie Foundation benefits, the mass production of Ph.D.'s became the order of the profession. This, in turn, raised the number of institutions qualified to grant doctorates—and the era of the graduate school was at hand. The production of Ph.D.'s zoomed from 615 in 1920 to 2,229 in 1930—and has continued to be a major industry.

The doctorate in philosophy—which was borrowed almost unthinkingly from the German model—did not necessarily have anything to do with philosophy as an area of study. The degree had originated, in medieval universities, as the award of the faculty of philosophy (as distinguished from those of arts and science, law, medicine, and theology). The university in the 19th and 20th centuries, however, developed its own elaborate system of graduate schools, all of which adopted the philosophy degree *in* history, mathematics, or whatever. Within the graduate schools were set up branches, called departments, and these were further subdivided almost to the point of absurdity. Again from Rudolph:

> Thus, in April 1893, the Department of Biology at the University of Chicago underwent an almost inevitable reorganization. Now instead of a Department of Biology there were five new departments: zoology, botany, anatomy, neurology, and physiology. And that meant five new departmental chairmanships, five new little hierarchies, five new competing domains of knowledge and ambition and interest. . . . Such multiplication of departments took place everywhere.

This kind of specialization had several by-products. One was an increasing narrowness of interest and approach, a kind of fragmentation of knowledge that defeated the declared purpose of liberal education—the sense of the continuity and interrelationship of all learning. Another was the absorption of professorial talent, not only in relative trivia, but also in departmental politicking and committee work. Educators began to lose sight of their task of demonstrating the relevance of what they taught, and turned their energies to working up details of an aspect of the compartment they had staked out. To protect this claim, they waged guerrilla warfare against their colleagues within the academic community for funds, facilities, assistants, and a share of the student enrollment. The cumulative effect of this rivalry resulted in a faculty that played a role in the administration of the institution, not with concern for the institution as a whole and its capacity to provide the best education possible, but to defend a niche and to advance segments of learning.

Weaning the Students

With the other German concepts that pervaded the educational scene appeared the notion that university students could and should provide for themselves. The fellows of the English colleges had felt obliged to mold the character and guard the morals of their charges, and the American colleges had adopted the doctrine of *in loco parentis* as suitable to the semiclerical environment of the early campus, on which almost all the students were in residence and for the first time deprived of parental care. The German universities, on the other hand, had taken over the tradition of the medieval universities on the Continent (where the college system failed to develop). As Metzger points out, it was assumed

> that German students were free to roam from place to place, sampling academic wares; that wherever they lighted, they were free to determine the choice and sequence of courses, and were responsible to no one for regular attendance; that they were exempted from all tests save the final examinations; that they lived in private quarters and controlled their private lives.

Although what was appropriate for mature graduates of a *Gymnasium* was not necessarily applicable to freshmen in the United States, the German university concept was more of a package than at first appeared. If students were capable of choosing their courses, why not let them choose their living quarters? And, as a matter of fact, since professors were increasingly reluctant to patrol dormitories and many of the student rebellions had been related to complaints about food and board, it was to be expected that the students' boarding house, the off-campus residence halls, and the fraternity chapters would find a ready welcome when they appeared soon after the Civil War.

Another link that was broken during the 19th century was that with the chapel. Although the colonial colleges had not been, as sometimes imagined, seminaries for the training of a clergy, the indoctrination of religious principles and practices had been universal and compulsory. Even during the anticlerical ripple of the Revolutionary period, students were shepherded to their prayers at regular intervals. Dixon Ryan Fox describes the scene at Union College:

> . . . the Chapel bell called sleepy boys to "repair in a decent and orderly manner" without running violently in the entries or down the stairs, to prayers that were to open the day. We can see the college butler on a cold pitch-black winter morning at his post beside the pulpit stairs, when the officers file in, holding his candle high so that the president may safely mount to read the scripture lesson . . . sure of each lad's attention, on penalty of a four-cent fine.

There was an occasional show of irreverence and even disorder. The trend, as the century progressed, was toward shorter and less frequent services, and the newly established universities, such as Johns Hopkins and Chicago, made chapel attendance voluntary. The first of the established institutions to abolish compulsory chapel was Wisconsin, in 1868; Harvard did not take the bold step until 1886.

The liberation of the student from dormitory and chapel, however gradual and partial—for some colleges retained and still retain the colonial pattern—was symbolic of a kind of permissiveness that characterized the era. (Historians usually prefer the term "laissez faire," which has a respectable 19th-century ring.) Actually, in a very large spectrum, students were permitted to do, outside of class, what interested them: culturally, in social activities, and in physical activities.

The first steps toward this permissiveness were taken during or soon after the colonial period, and the trend gathered strength before the Civil War. In the era between the Civil War and World War I, the spread between curricular and extracurricular activities began to alarm part of the academic community; Princeton's Woodrow Wilson wondered if the "side shows" might not have "swallowed up the circus." However, it was realized that the new customers for college were of a slightly different breed than in earlier times. They were still an elite, the sons and daughters of the top 5 to 10 per cent in the economic scale, who did not depend on their college education to provide them with jobs. But neither Jacksonian America nor Reconstruction America held with the gentleman's code, with its obligations toward society, that characterized comparable British circles (and, to some degree, the colonies). The young graduates expected to have good jobs in business or banking or a lucrative profession, which would be provided by the same families that could afford to dispense with their services for the college years. While at their studies, classroom work could give them some useful information, no doubt, but it was expected to give them "polish" (the 19th-century substitute for the 18th-century "character") and connections. Meanwhile, they were only young once. The campus became their playground.

To begin with culture, it must be said that the students

learned very early that the curriculum was not likely to offer them much that was meaningful. During the years when the English Romantic poets were producing works that would enthrall adolescents a century later, no college in the United States had a course in contemporary English literature. Philosophy classes knew nothing of Kant. The next generation did not study Schopenhauer, nor did they find Dickens or Scott in the college libraries. Amherst tried in vain to have English literature taught in the 1820's. Even American history made its Harvard debut only in 1838.

The void was at least partly filled by the students, who adapted the medieval tradition of the disputation, through the Commencement oration, into the debate. In the late colonial years, students used this unpromising vehicle of communication to exchange ideas on current topics. The debating society, in turn, became the literary society, which swept the campuses during the early republican period. According to Brubacher and Rudy, it "commanded the kind of passionate student loyalty which was later accorded to fraternities and athletic teams." In fact, elections to these societies were bitterly contested, and several of the early Greek-letter fraternities originated as tactical groupings in literary society election campaigns.

Aside from providing an outlet for the intellectual energy of the students, the literary societies proved transitional. Without them, the campuses would have been even more sterile than they were. The major contemporary "radicals"— such men as Wendell Phillips and Ralph Waldo Emerson— were unwelcome at the colleges, but the literary societies provided them with platforms. College libraries were kept under lock, and included little of interest to students beyond their classroom assignments. So the debating and literary societies accumulated books, and before the Civil War their libraries were often larger and always more used than those of the institutions. Another bequest of the literary societies was the student publication, which flourished independently long after the last society had been overwhelmed by the fraternity system. For it was the Greek-letter club, with its accent on social rather than cultural activity, that attracted extracurricular interest after the Civil War.

Purely social clubs had existed much earlier—Harvard's Porcellian and Hasty Pudding clubs originated in the colonial and Revolutionary periods. Such societies had been built mainly on snob appeal, and this characteristic of the Greek-letter societies was one basis for criticism soon after their appearance. Another was the secrecy associated with some of the "lodges"—a feature that repelled many from the Masonic lodges as well, after a defector from the Masonic movement, who was prepared to "tell all," was murdered in 1826.

The first Greek-letter chapter was that of Phi Beta Kappa at William and Mary, in 1776. Fifty years later, when this society—with chapters on a number of campuses—changed from a social to an honor fraternity, a new group of social Greek-letter chapters appeared at Union College in New York. By 1850 there were 16 such societies, all at private institutions. The fraternities had rough going in the state institutions, where neither snobbism nor secrecy was popular with legislators. The outlawing of fraternities at such institutions was eventually upheld by the U.S. Supreme Court, and a number of private colleges and universities also banned the societies.

Yet, despite constant hostility from many directions, the Greek-letter movement grew and thrived. It apparently served several needs on the 19th-century campus. Many of the students wanted to group themselves socially according to their own interests, and if these were sometimes snobbish, the students were only following the example of their parents. The increasing number of girls on college campuses augmented social activity in general. The movement away from the dormitories made the chapter house or lodge an attractive solution, preferable to the boarding house, for the problem of living quarters. There could be no more ideal place to meet future business associates, political cronies, or marriage partners than in the fraternity and sorority house. Membership in cliques, which seemed shameful to some of the critics, was precisely what many parents desired for their sons and daughters; it reflected the society for which, surely, college was preparing them.

It is not surprising that the competitive spirit of the 19th-century United States should find its reflection in the development of organized athletics. Nevertheless, a hostile tradition had first to be overcome. As at the medieval university, so at the colonial college, students had been discouraged from displaying athletic tendencies. Rudolph cites, from a history of Rensselaer Polytechnic Institute, a typical official precept posted in the 1820's:

> Such exercises as running, jumping, climbing, scuffling, and the like are calculated to detract from that dignity of deportment which becomes a man of science.

Yet, within that same decade, a flurry of approved calisthenics did appear on a few campuses. Its origin was traced to the early German immigrants, who began to arrive in even greater numbers in the 1840's and who imported an expanded gymnastic program. This activity became legitimate when it was viewed, not as mere sport, but as body-building, and in the years preceding the Civil War gymnastics was accepted on campuses from Virginia to Bowdoin to Oberlin. One Virginia student is quoted by Rudolph as objecting that the regimen "is so business-like, that exercise ceases to be a pleasure and becomes a labor. Where are the sports that become a great university . . . ? Where are our cricket matches?"

The University of Pennsylvania actually did organize a cricket team in 1843. But somehow boating became more popular, and in 1853 a Harvard crew beat a Yale crew on Lake Winnepesaukee in New Hampshire. Both cricket and rowing were English imports—Oxford had rowed against Cambridge since 1829, and Lord's had for many years seen cricket matches between the universities and between Eton and Harrow as well. But in 1859 a game that was essentially American, baseball, made its collegiate debut at Pittsfield, Massachusetts, where Amherst played Williams. There was even some frolicking with footballs on some campuses before the Civil War, but the games were more like soccer than the sport of the current gridiron, even when Princeton tied Rutgers in a two-game series in 1869.

In 1873 Cornell's President Andrew Dickson White wired Michigan's team: "I will not permit thirty men to travel four hundred miles merely to agitate a bag of wind." This proved the least prophetic statement ever uttered publicly by White. The American adaptation of England's rugby swept the campuses within a decade—and remained spectacularly a college sport. Its impact transcended the playing fields. Long before colleges were able to agree on standards of curriculum or entrance requirements, they met to iron out playing rules. The faculty was forced to recognize the competition of the coach—and eventually to admit physical education as a duly recognized academic department. The football scholarship began to enroll students who might not otherwise have been able to seek a degree. Football heroes outranked mental giants and social paragons. Football games drew throngs that provided unanticipated revenues during the season, and successful teams inspired alumni to donate recklessly. Legislators also were impressed and became quick to release funds to state colleges with champion "aggregations." A number of small private colleges, incapable of producing Ph.D.'s, made a comeback by building a stable of football stars.

A few schools, such as Columbia and Stanford, were shocked by the mounting list of casualties on the field and temporarily suspended the contests, but in 1905 the forward pass was devised to mitigate the slaughter, and the colleges formed an athletic association to police the sport. Intramural contests were organized, and enthusiasm for intercollegiate athletics became as mandatory as patriotism. According to Everett Lee Hunt, historian of Swarthmore, that institution's student journal, the *Phoenix,* rejoiced at the reinstatement of the game, citing

the numbers of governors, senators, judges, ambassadors, mayors, attorneys general, and industrialists who had played football. The student paper repeated quotations from many of these men to the effect that football had been the strongest influence in preparing them for public leadership.

Thus there developed, on the 19th-century campus, and projecting into the 20th century, a "collegiate" mode. The chores of the classroom were subdued. Feverish activity appeared in rushing and pledging, in hazing, in playing games or watching them and "rooting" for the home team. Ambition concentrated on such matters as meeting the right classmates and winning favorable notices in the class book. Alan Valentine, a Swarthmore dean, describes the era of his own undergraduate days in his autobiography:

> The "all-around man" was the most popular while in college and the most likely to be offered a good job on graduation. [He] wanted success; college and society were teaching him what success was, and the practical ways of getting it. . . . The quest for personal standing should precede the quest for the welfare of society. All this was in the atmosphere one breathed. . . . In rather different ways than its Faculty intended, the college prepared its students for the century they would live in, where one could be successful without ideas and happy without excellence if one accepted majority opinion and got on well with people of one's kind.

This era of conformity, which burgeoned into full glory with the 1920's (Dean Valentine's school days), had been developing for half a century or more—a period in which there were no significant campus revolts. Athletic activities, in particular, have been credited with siphoning off energies and keeping mischief to the level of pranks and panty raids. But it seems more probable that these were generations of young people who enjoyed their campus interlude between childhood and "real life." The pseudo-medieval rite of Commencement bridged the generation gap between the big man on campus and the nostalgic alumnus. The students were rarely critical either of the diversions afforded them as collegians or of the society they were being groomed to lead.

One device that prepared them for their leadership role may be described as "student government." According to Ruth Strang, in *Group Activities in College and Secondary Schools,* published in 1941:

> The earlier aim was to relieve the masters of details; more recently, the aim has been to supply educational experiences of value to the students, out of which will grow increasing self-direction and self-control on their part.

This evaluation suggests the direction of the movement rather more convincingly than its accomplishments. There had been several very early attempts to involve students in some aspects of self-administration, but none had succeeded or left a tradition that could be built on. The students at William and Mary had elected representatives to a central organization in 1779; the same college had experimented with faculty autonomy; but neither innovation could be sustained. Amherst and the University of Virginia tried to turn over some cases of student discipline to student "courts" in the 1820's, but these efforts were also without success. Jefferson, particularly, hoped that students could be permitted to govern themselves, in the European tradition, with a student-elected proctor provided with legal status. But the American students were neither as old nor as accustomed to self-discipline as their European counterparts, and Virginia legislators would not accept the novel concept of a university court.

Oberlin, with its totally unconventional approach, provided some opportunities for student participation in college management; so did the University of Michigan for a while, and the Evanston College for Ladies (which later became part of Northwestern University). There was considerable variation in the degree of power allowed to the students and the scope over which this power could be exercised, but it was usually limited to mediation between the student population and the faculty or administration, or to specific areas of discipline, such as various buildings or parts of buildings used by the students. The so-called honor system was generally under student auspices. According to the authors of a study of student activities, A. O. Bowden and Ida C. Clarke, early in the 1920's three-fifths of the colleges they reported on had some form of honor system; four-fifths had compulsory-membership student organizations. At that time was organized the National Self-Government Committee, Inc., which was succeeded in the 1930's by the National Student Federation, a body described by Gordon J. Klopf in *College Student Government* as "a loosely knit federation of student governments . . . which met annually and discussed the organization and principles of student government." All these were progenitors of the National Student Association, founded in 1946.

Student government was admired by some educators for various reasons: as a character builder, as a laboratory for civics in action or public speaking, even as a lightning rod for the disaffected. Some students found satisfaction in campus politics, but others compared the student "senates" to company unions, and when the storms broke on campus the rods failed to deflect the bolts.

CHAPTER FIVE

THE CHANGING ROLE OF THE UNIVERSITY

AN ENTIRELY NEW ERA began for the American colleges and universities after World War I, when the United States and its role in the world were transformed. As a world power, however reluctant, the country was faced with new political and economic ideas that had not appeared in most college curricula up to that time—socialism, communism, and soon several variations of fascism. These ideas could safely be ignored during the dozen prosperous years that immediately followed World War I, but the sudden collapse of a thriving economy raised questions demanding serious study.

American workers and farmers and millions of unemployed asked the cause of their plight, and American intellectuals—who were humiliated and angry, not only because they ate less, but because they felt betrayed—began to reexamine ancient values. World War II ended the Depression but did not answer the questions or restore traditional patterns. Moreover, the malaise did not end with the formal conflict. Students, among others, thought they had a right to know whether and why they should prepare for a new holocaust —especially since there would obviously be no opportunity to ask questions once the Bomb fell.

The Depression and World War II changed the essence of American life in many respects, allowing—or compelling— the national government and powerful industrial combinations to intervene in areas that had always been the preserve of private citizens or local governments. It had become clear, for example, that neither the immediate care of the destitute nor the shoring up of the wrecked economy could be entrusted to "charity" or barter programs or community ingenuity—although all these were tried. One after another, institutions that had foundered and clogged the economic channels were salvaged and once more set afloat, and eventually returned to traditional tacks. But the institutions of higher learning never sought or required aid, and the principle of local control of education continued to prevail without challenge.

The colleges and universities weathered the Depression and the war with pennants flying. In the lean years, young men and women who were unemployed somehow managed to continue their studies in almost normal numbers. Although a degree failed to command a job, lack of a degree could assure almost certain unemployment in many fields. So another half-million students were added to the college rolls between 1930 and 1945. After the war, the GI's camped—sometimes with their wives—on the campuses, pushing the existing institutions into expansive gestures that would soon prove inadequate.

The population growth, between 1916 and 1946, was in itself phenomenal, completing the irreversible shift from the

farms to the cities. The three decades saw a fourfold increase of students on the campuses (excluding the GI's);
and one-fifth of the high school graduates in 1946 (compared with one-sixteenth in 1916) sought degrees. Twenty
years later, the enrollment had quadrupled once more—
from 1,600,000 in college to 6,000,000. By this time, almost half the high school students were matriculating.

The statistics are impressive, but the story they tell has
several possible interpretations. Half the youngsters of high
school age were going to high school in 1930; by 1968
more than three-quarters were going to high school and
almost half the youth of college age were going to college.
This can be called "democratization," meaning that a higher
level of education is offered to a larger part of the eligible
population. But it can also be called "cultural inflation."
Once the high school diploma had been a virtual requirement for jobs of a certain category. Now most of these
jobs require a baccalaureate. It takes a master's or better to
get the job that once was available to a mere college graduate.

The student with "aspirations" must walk up the down
escalator. Of all the degrees granted in 1946, 12 per cent
were master's and 1.2 per cent doctor's degrees. Twenty
years later the proportion had almost doubled: to 20 per
cent and 2 per cent respectively. In fact, more masters entered "real life" in 1967 than bachelors in 1930. This
remorseless pressure turned the campus into an assembly
line for the graduate school. It became advisable for high
school youngsters to decide whether they would try to climb
the rigid educational ladder to the top, or whether they
would settle for the kind of career available to graduates of

high school plus two to four years of college and an associate or bachelor's degree.

The Options

The very need to make such a choice—to think in terms of training for a job rather than getting an education for living—undercut the liberal arts idea and put in its place a vocational-professional program. The college-bound youth of the 20th century could find institutions of almost any type—providing an old-fashioned classical education, or job training at any level, or an endless supply of fact and theory on any subject to any depth. What he could not find, however, was the judgment to select, from this educational supermarket-plus-specialty shop, the items or the regimen best suited to his own capabilities.

Any educational system that serves 6,000,000 students (the prospect for 1985 is about 10,000,000) and comprises a variety of institutions can hardly be characterized in a sentence or a paragraph. But the contemporary American system of higher education does seem to relate to its students in a fairly specific manner: It proposes to certify them as capable of assuming a certain role in society, according to the rung of the educational ladder at which they drop off. (In this sense, it is not so different from the medieval university, which symbolized its accreditation to society by conferring the *biretta.*) According to Daniel Bell, in *The Reforming of General Education,* those who achieve the doctorate from one of the top twenty universities have made it:

A higher degree with creditable work from one of the elite universities has become a passport to a position in one of these universities, to a place in the major research laboratories, and to an administrative position in government.

A lesser degree, or a higher degree at a lesser institution, leads to an assignment lower down on the totem pole. The penalty for failing to achieve a bachelor's is well understood, and is softened by the award of a consolation associate degree. The student is, in effect, put through a filter or sieve, like a crop of peas at the cannery. But there is little doubt, as Christopher Jencks and David Riesman point out in *The Academic Revolution,* that "the crucial raison d'être of the American college . . . may not be education but certification."

Many choices seem to be open to the high school graduate, but this is an illusion. For in the end it is not the student who chooses, but the institution. Admission to an elite university, or to one of the elite four-year colleges that serve as feeders to an elite university, is cruelly limited. The criterion is seldom "what the college might do for the student" but "what the student is likely to do for the college," and this is based on high school performance. (As a result, high schools jealous of their reputations for placement in good colleges have a rugged curriculum.) Of more than 2,000 institutions of higher learning, only about 7 per cent are universities, and only about 1 per cent are elite universities.

The next option is one of the less desirable universities or one of the four-year colleges that feed them. There are hundreds of mediocre (or worse) colleges and hundreds of "professional schools" of all varieties and standards to serve those who will settle for a B.A. or a B.S. And the fastest-growing type of institution, taking the overflow of high school graduates who still have hopes, is the community or junior college, which provides an academic niche for two years and a chance, always a chance, that some four-year college will have an opening in its junior class (since about half the entering freshmen of four-year colleges drop out without graduating).

The spectacular enrollments have, in fact, placed the colleges in a position comparable to that of the secondary schools in the late 19th century. American youth considers it a right (and a necessity) to enroll in college, not a privilege. But there is an important difference between the absorptive capacity of the colleges and that of the high schools of an earlier generation.

With the spread of the high schools as part of the public school system, the academies withered away, and only a relative handful of private schools (some of them very prestigious) survived. But the private colleges and universities will not follow the academies into oblivion. For higher education is not by any means part of the free public school system. There is little likelihood that the taxpayers will assume that burden, although the number of state universities, state colleges, municipal institutions, and community colleges will continue to grow. The budget for a tuition-free full-fledged university system to enroll more than 90 per cent of the nation's youth would be astronomical. Other programs—the war on poverty, for example—are even more pressing.

So the existing institutions are in an enviable position. Some have chosen to maintain their old-fashioned charm, with an intimate and gracious campus bordered by fraternity houses, selected social and cultural activities, a curriculum modern and advanced enough to graduate first-rate candidates for higher degrees at elite universities, a superior and relaxed teaching staff, and a vestige of concern about students' morals and character. Fewer than 1 per cent of the nation's students attend such institutions. At the other end of the spectrum are the multiversities—to use a term coined by Clark Kerr. There are only about two dozen of these colossal institutions. They share with the serene academic oases just described one feature: They are equally selective in their admissions policies. But the small colleges finance this privilege by charging high tuitions; the multiversities require other sources of revenue—and the cultivation of these sources has had the effect of reshaping the entire system of higher education.

New Uses for Universities

The most obvious characteristic of the multiversity is its huge student population—enrollment at the University of California approached 95,000 on ten campuses in 1967. It follows that the institution has a gigantic physical plant, a complex administrative staff, an enormous and unwieldy conglomeration of faculties, and a budget fit for a kingdom. Such an apparatus is not allowed to develop simply for the purpose of providing instruction to young men and women; far more efficient and economical forms of organization are capable of performing that function. On the other hand, the multiversity was not actually created to do the job it has undertaken. It developed, or evolved, out of the 19th-century-type university.

The feature of that earlier university that distinguished

it from the simpler college was, of course, the graduate
school–an adjunct to the college at which the bachelor
could supplement his education by acquiring more specialized
(especially professional) knowledge, and the professor could
enrich his teaching by research and in so doing add to the
sum of knowledge. The ideal situation would have been an
equilibrium between these two functions of teaching and
research. But such a balance, if it was ever achieved, could
not be sustained. The implacable flood of knowledge, which
the university helped to swell, in turn inundated the university.

Modern scholars, in awe at what they have accomplished, find it as difficult to define the scale of their
activities as a space-age astronomer measuring cosmic dis-
tances in terms of miles. What is the equivalent of the
light-year or the parsec in the field of knowledge expansion? Only a computer could (and does) assimilate the
available data. Columbia's Daniel Bell points out that every
50 years since 1750 the number of scientific journals (then
ten) has multiplied tenfold–which would yield 100,000
by 1950. To bring the accumulated information within
reach of those who need it, the abstract was developed,
summarizing the contents of larger works. But by 1950
there were already 300 abstract journals, each running to
more than 10,000 pages. Bell estimates that "in the physical
and life sciences the number of books add up to about
60,000 annually, the number of research reports to about
100,000, and the number of articles in scientific and technical journals to about 1.2 million each year." If this
account is compared to an astronomer's glance at "our"
galaxy, consider what remains to be learned as the scientific

spacemen rocket into and past the countless other galaxies of knowledge. A score of years ago it was possible to classify personnel in the fields of science and technology into 50 distinct specializations; now there are more than 900 such categories. Only a university with the most sophisticated equipment and staff could conceivably explore, or even chart, what has become essential to operate the modern world.

The universities possessed some equipment relevant to the task. They had long since set up a departmental organization based on the specialization of each branch of knowledge. This departmentalization was found useful in defining the interest, or competence, of the professors—their "disciplines," in academic jargon—but the relationship of each discipline to others became more difficult to recognize as the edifice of knowledge added superstructures and wings and garrets and subcellars. It then became customary to preserve the identity of one discipline by emphasizing the manner in which it differed from adjacent disciplines, rather than by knocking down the partitions between them—for this would lead to chaos. It was easier to subdivide a given discipline (e.g., geology into mineralogy, stratigraphy, geomorphology, etc.), allowing the researcher to concentrate his interest, than to fuse disciplines that are obviously related (geochemistry and biochemistry, for example). But although such fusion irritates some researchers, the situations outside the laboratories seldom conform to disciplines.

Although the setting up of compartmented disciplines in a kind of federal association (the university) did little to reflect phenomena occurring in the real world, it did make possible an apparatus for the organization of knowledge and the efficient conduct of research. It just happened that at this juncture in American development a great need existed for just such an apparatus. On the other hand, there was a well-established precedent for diverting the educational institutions from their primary task of teaching the young.

The land-grant concept had made the university a legitimate community resource. If Wisconsin could use the laboratories and staff of its state university to advantage, there was no reason why the Federal government should not utilize the nation's ivy-clad workshops and certified intellectuals to tackle the variety of problems that intensified during the Depression years.

Actually, the universities had been involved—through their emissaries to Washington, popularly known as "egg-heads"—during the Roosevelt Administration. Then, as the war approached its end, the Federal government turned to the academic community for help in applying the theory of atom-splitting to building the Bomb. The contrasts are startling in the leap from the Wisconsin idea, which established a flourishing dairy industry, to the Manhattan Project, which made possible a balance of terror. But on a less cosmic level, the event signified the presence of government on campus, at first as a guest and before long—it might be argued—as a trespasser.

In 1963 Clark Kerr told a Harvard audience that Federal support "has already changed the face of the leading American universities almost as much as did the land-grant program a century earlier." He was understating the case, for the Morrill program had merely pointed the way and was only slowly adopted, whereas the postwar universities rushed headlong into the embrace of government and government-allied industry. According to figures cited by Kerr, the Federal government increased its stake in higher education a hundredfold—from $15 million to $1.5 billion—in the years 1940–1960 spanning the hot and cold wars. In 1960, $1 billion went for research, and this sum took care of three-fourths of all the research done by the universities and provided one-seventh of all the funds received by all universities in that year.

It must not be thought that the Treasurer of the United States took on the posture of Elihu Yale or even John D. Rockefeller. The pattern of involvement was complex, obscure, or even secret—as is to be expected, since much (though not all) of the research had "defense" applications. Some laboratories—such as Chicago's Argonne or Caltech's Jet Propulsion Lab—were built with Federal money and are managed by a single private institution; others—such as Brookhaven—are operated by a consortium of universities. The latter form is also used for so-called institutes, such as the controversial Institute for Defense Analyses. The government-funded and university-operated institute has appeared in other areas, sometimes disguised. University services have been used by such bureaus as the Agency for International Development, and universities have received Central Intelligence Agency money to plan and staff intervention in the internal affairs of foreign countries. In 1968 a project under the "guidance" of Michigan State University and AID, intended to improve the curriculum of the University of Guatemala, was attacked and abandoned because some students thought it concealed a CIA plot. Sometimes events lend unexpected significance to routine projects, or "pure" research ripens for application, and funds begin to flow. Thus, Robert S. Morison recounts how certain institutes concerned with "exotic" languages were dramatically spotlighted during World War II, when they "provided the background for the intensive studies of a series of relatively unknown tongues to meet military needs." In the cold war years, institutes of Russian and then Chinese studies flowered on a hundred campuses. A government-university team investigated Unidentified Flying Objects at the University of Colorado. More recently, the "plight of the cities" and African studies have become thriving subject areas. Whatever needs research can find a campus willing and able to accept a properly funded assignment. Research and development—good old R & D—may flourish in big business hothouses, but the seed is best developed in the universities, which have a virtual monopoly on what Kerr describes as "the knowledge industry":

> Knowledge has certainly never in history been so central to the conduct of an entire society. What the railroads did for the second half of the last century and the automobile for the first half of this century may be done for the second half of this century by the knowledge industry: that is, to serve as the focal point for national growth. And the university is at the center of the knowledge process.

The Academic Entrepreneur

Another kind of service is provided by the university: the use of its staff. According to Hugh S. Brown and Lewis B. Mayhew, in *American Higher Education:*

> . . . a growing number of professors receive grants and contracts from philanthropic and governmental organiza-

tions to support research. The funding agent either supports the professor in studying what he wants to study or pays him to do research of interest to the agency.

In such a situation, the smart professor may well choose to work in a field likely to be attractive to a philanthropic or governmental (or commercial) organization. Moreover, he is likely to seek a place to work that will provide him with facilities, including not only library and laboratory, but also a supporting staff of graduate students. The educational argument is: They learn while they help him with research; he is a better teacher because his research takes him out of the ivory tower and into the real live world. The institution may also benefit, because a staff of much-sought-after researchers adds to its reputation, and may bring additional grants, which afford funds that build more library and laboratory facilities. These, in turn, attract more ambitious researchers (faculty and graduate student), and so on.

The benefit to the institution, however, is by no means as certain as that to the star researcher. In practice, Federal grants often accrue to the individual rather than to the institution, and frequently when a researcher moves to another institution, his grants follow him.

The picture emerges of a new kind of professor who may use his campus office as a headquarters but spends much of his working time with politicians, business executives, and the military brass. The "brain trust" is neither legend nor, any longer, folk humor. Society has found that it cannot function without either the university or the professor-on-loan.

Perhaps one portrait, among many supplied by James

Ridgeway in an article in *Harper's,* will provide a sense of reality. It is that of a professor at Harvard Business School who helped the U.S. Navy with purchasing problems during World War II, and whose help continued after the war. "Since the dean thought it improper to continue this business through the school," a company was organized for which "Harvard and MIT professors served as consultants." During the Korean War, the company grossed $1,500,000 annually, although the professor continued on the Business School faculty. He sold his share in the company, which "again relied heavily on professors from Harvard and MIT, as well as Stanford. This company helped the Navy, Air Force, and NASA develop ways to keep tabs on weapons and missile systems, and it too had an annual income of about $3 million. . . ." The professor again sold his interest, remaining as consultant, and founded another institute with offices in Boston, New York, and Washington. He "put together this assortment of companies very much as a new university might assemble a faculty." (It is some kind of milestone, when business takes lessons in organization from the professors.) One of the companies in the institute was owned by a Boston University professor; another by a Harvard psychologist who, with his graduate students and protégés, became part of a "science center" that helps, among others, Navy chaplains, fraternity leaders, and life insurance executives in their respective functions.

Not all of the entrepreneur professors are as picturesquely successful or adjusted to the requirements of the world around them. But the type is not rare in the major universities, and it is in a strategic position. Another student of the contemporary university, John Fischer, believes these pro-

fessors can use their influence—based on the prestige and
funds they can draw to their institutions—to "reshape the
university." There is no doubt at all that they are able to
pick their institutions and, with this kind of bargaining
power, dictate their conditions of employment. Naturally,
they teach little, if at all, and the students in their circle
of influence are likely to be assistants and apprentices rather
than scholars. What is more, there is likely to be heavy
competition for the privilege of entering this circle.

Clark Kerr, who was in a position to know, has described very clearly a possible impact of the mercenary researcher (although he does not so characterize him):

> Some faculty members come to use the pressure of their
> agency contacts against their university. They may try to
> force the establishment of a new administrative unit or the
> assignment of land for their own special building . . .
> some faculty members tend to shift their identification and
> loyalty from their university to the agency . . . [which]
> becomes the new alma mater.

A less obvious, though perhaps a more prevalent, tendency
on the part of the faculty seems to be the transfer of allegiance from the institution, not to an agency or other
employer in connection with moonlighting ventures, but
to their discipline. They easily hop from one institution to
another, and wage valiant combat in the councils of each on
behalf of their own department and against all competitors.
The end result is that in matters curricular such professors
are thoroughly conservative; and in matters concerning the
university as a whole, they are narrowly parochial. They
accept enough committee work to defend their departmental
interest, but they begrudge the time consumed by such

work and are reluctant to take on further committee work for the welfare of the institution itself. They are uninterested in "faculty power." The path from the medieval guild of scholars ends at the department chairman's door. Students do not enter.

The contemporary professor is also likely to have a characteristic relationship to students. His primary interest must be in research, for on this his reputation in the scholarly world—and usually his wage scale—depends. This is a fact not only because his commodity, knowledge or expertise, currently fetches a high price on the market, but because respect for scholarship has been distorted into a fetish, epitomized by the doctrine of "Publish or Perish."

Professors sometimes deplore this situation, but they are not blameless. At first they struggled to naturalize in the United States such privileges as the dignity of their calling and academic freedom. Then they became discipline-conscious (or obsessed) and began writing for scholarly journals those billions of words a year addressed to one another. This mechanism provides a convenient word-count and satisfies a need: Teachers grade students, alumni keep tally of football victories, and trustees compute publication credits. It would be less convenient to evaluate teaching effectiveness—one must wait until the taught have demonstrated the effect of the teachings. (One recalls that Socrates left no writings.)

Few university teachers—unlike grade school teachers—have been specifically trained for their alleged profession. Paul Goodman, who does not concede that college teaching *is* a profession, points out in *Community of Scholars* that an elementary schoolteacher teaches a person (the child), not a subject; a high school instructor teaches a person (the adolescent) by means of a subject; for the college professor, the emphasis is on the subject, not the person (the student). It is in this subject area alone that the professor has been certified through the doctorate. He has not acquired any skill in transmitting whatever he may know. What is worse, he is not certain to have any real interest in this aspect of his work.

A very large percentage of older teachers—especially those who move from campus to campus—make a lower teaching "load" a prime point in bargaining. In his introduction to a group of papers entitled *The Contemporary University*, Robert S. Morison says that "many of the best men are in 'contact' with students for as little as three hours a week." These students are certain to be in graduate school, where the professors also take some time off from research to hear Ph.D. orals and read master's dissertations. Bell reports of his own Columbia College: ". . . since a professor will usually give a graduate lecture course and a research seminar in his subject, he may thus have no time for College teaching." He adds that the graduate assistants who take over the lecture sections, discussion groups, and quizzes "have detailed knowledge of a particular specialty acquired in recent graduate work but are less qualified for the broader general education courses. . . ." In all fairness it must be noted that Jencks and Riesman report another conclusion:

> . . . while the teaching assistants who fill in for those senior men who flee the classroom are often deprecated by status-conscious undergraduates, they frequently know more than senior faculty and in the better places also care more.

Detour: General Education and Junior College

More than 6,000,000 young men and women compete frantically for openings in more than 2,000 institutions of higher learning. At the small proportion of these institutions having the highest reputations—the most potent career launching-pads—they are processed through an apparatus no longer structured to serve them. Educators and experts in matters academic rarely agree on many points, but there is virtual unanimity on this: The primary usefulness of the modern multiversity is not for the undergraduate, is only indirectly for the graduate student, and is increasingly on behalf of counterpart organizations of industry and government, equally sophisticated and complexly structured.

The intimacy between great institutions of higher learning and great corporations or government bureaus is made easy by the circumstance that they very often share a common staff. Even in colonial days it was customary for some of the trustees of most of the colleges of importance to be *ex officio* politicos—governors, state treasurers, legislators. The seats of the clerical trustees were eventually filled by pillars of the church in nonclerical garb, who could be counted on to advance policies, educational and budgetary, acceptable to the secular Establishment. So it came to pass that the modern version of the governing board, under whatever name, comprises very solid citizens. Corporation directors, bankers, top-drawer lawyers, realtors, retired military brass, press lords, are appointed by legislators or chosen by alumni or co-opt one another, and gather in conclave one or two times a month to oversee the institutions. They set up a functioning administration to take over the routine of running the establishment in precisely the same manner, though with less intrinsic concern, as they operate their own enterprises. This relieves the teaching staff of considerable administrative detail and frees them for scholarly research, service to society, and a certain amount of teaching.

The first intimations that higher education was side-tracking some of its instructional chores could be detected in that 19th-century debate between the defenders of liberal arts and the enthusiasts for curricular innovations. The arts advocates often made the mistake of pleading for an out-worn program with arguments that were equally stale—that such a program of classics had always proved beneficial and rewarding, or that the untried could prove disrupting or frivolous. But the advancement of learning was inexorable, and much of it was in the physical and (later) the social sciences—areas that invited application to real-life situations and were consistent with the trend toward vocational and professional education.

Latin ceased to be the language used by commencement valedictorians; even diplomas were inscribed in English; and at Columbia, Bell pointed out that the striking of Latin as an entrance requirement to that college in 1916 made possible the admission of previously excluded public school graduates and changed the "ethnic and social composition" of the institution. This may symbolize one aspect of the defeat of the classicists. The victory of the innovators, who claimed to be fostering an academic revolution, can be symbolized in catalogues that look like telephone books; students can shop for courses through the "yellow pages," and, according to Brubacher and Rudy, "it became possible for students to turn in their credits like clipping so many coupons to get a degree."

The supermarket syndrome disturbed some educators as

soon as it appeared. One approach to counteract it, without reverting to obsolete practices, was to provide guidance for the bewildered students. If they were to become consumers, at least let them be discriminating and purposeful consumers. Johns Hopkins and Harvard made the first gestures in the last decades of the 19th century, and the guideposts appeared on campus after campus in the years after World War I. Says Rudolph:

> By the 1920's most colleges and universities were busy perfecting various systems of freshman counselling, freshman week, faculty advisers, and before long the campus psychologist as well as the college chaplain would join these many agencies in giving organized expression to a purpose that had once been served most simply by a dedicated faculty.

Another approach was the reinstatement of the tutor, in one capacity or another. Woodrow Wilson, as president of Princeton in 1905, had tried to bridge the gap between lecturing professors and note-taking students by using tutors, called preceptors, to conduct less formal discussion groups. President Frank Aydelotte of Swarthmore developed the "honors system" (not to be confused with the "honor system" of taking tests without supervision) in order to combat the leveling-down aspects of the formal curriculum. "Brighter" students, with the help of tutors, could depart from the routine and set their own pace. Harvard's President A. Lawrence Lowell, in a valiant effort to unscramble the omelet, tried to motivate undergraduates to organize the chaos of cultural goodies set before them. They faced a final "general examination" that would test their capacity to discover an over-all relationship among the contents of

their freely elected courses—and this was intended to en-
courage a less random selection of those courses. In this
gentle about-face from the elective system, it was found
necessary to supply tutors, and the entire faculty was mo-
bilized for the task. On this rock the new Cambridge
foundered—the regular faculty had other, to them more
rewarding, tasks than to wet-nurse undergraduates.

There were other efforts to discover viable new patterns.
At Reed College, founded just before World War I, it was
decided to concentrate on learning by prohibiting the dis-
tractions of the extracurriculum. Venerable Antioch, 68
years after its founding, took the radical step of alternating
work and classroom activity for its students, hoping that
each would enrich the other. The gesture was admired but
not imitated. Several small and respected women's colleges
in the East—notably Sarah Lawrence and Bennington—experimented with programs that rewarded creativity, imagina-
tion, and the individual relish of selected cultural areas.
This approach stimulated an elite and was appreciated, but
was far from the mainstream of higher education in the
1920's and 1930's.

The swan song of the well-intentioned reformers was
uttered by A. Lawrence Lowell:

> . . . the college ought to produce not defective specialists
> but men intellectually well-rounded, of wide sympathies and
> unfettered judgment. At the same time they ought to be
> trained to hard and accurate thought, and this . . . re-
> quires a mastery of something, acquired by continuous
> application. Surely the essence of a liberal education con-
> sists of an attitude of mind, a familiarity with methods
> of thought, an ability to use information rather than in a

memory stocked with facts, however valuable such a store-house may be.

A more determined and enduring offensive against the fragmented curriculum was the movement labeled "general education." It was, curiously enough, hatched from a martial egg—a course at Columbia College during World War I to train a corps of student officers (forerunners of the ROTC) on the subject of War Issues. It occurred to a few professors that such a potpourri might be adapted to peacetime uses. If we needed orientation to fight the German Kaiser, perhaps we could use some to face the complex problems of a postwar world. Thus, in 1917, every Columbia freshman was compelled to take Contemporary Civilization five days a week. Later comparable "survey" or "interdisciplinary" courses were prepared in the Humanities and Sciences, and they were adapted in one form or another at colleges and universities all over the country. Some are still operating.

The rationale was that specialization had, indeed, got out of hand. The departmental structure that had overwhelmed the graduate schools crept back into the undergraduate schools and sidewise into the feeder institutions. A language "major" could get entangled in French linguistics and literature, without ever studying French history (which places the rest in perspective). A physicist could probe comfortably in the world of subnuclear particles but remain utterly innocent of the consequences for the world of what he was doing—until, like a few of the alumni of Los Alamos, he read articles by scientists of other disciplines about the effects of fallout.

Columbia and its imitators proposed to restore, at some point, a period in the undergraduate program for thoughtful reflection, for an overlook across the cultural landscape before the plunge into the undergrowth. And even in a committee report of 1946 there could be detected a vestige of the old school spirit:

> In the meaning of liberal arts we include all studies that contribute to the art of living, as distinct from the channeled preparation of making a living.

An independent development of the concept of general education took place at the University of Chicago. Two presidents of that university, with contrasting views concerning the role of the institution, shared in the experiment, and although the effort was not crowned with success, it brought forward a new kind of institution that may deflect the direction of higher education in the United States.

It had long been obvious that many colleges were actually offering high school courses in the freshman year; this had become a subject of complaint among freshmen who had graduated from secondary schools having high standards. To solve this problem, some colleges had made a practice of advancing such students directly to the sophomore year on entrance. The question inevitably arose: What is sacred about the traditional "4-4" schedule: four years in secondary school followed by four years in college?

At the turn of the century, President Harper of Chicago had sought to challenge the 4-4 pattern. His motive was the development of the graduate facilities of the university, and he hoped to advance this by sloughing off the "junior college," as he termed the freshman and sophomore years.

With the example of the *Gymnasium* in mind, Harper encouraged a number of high schools in the Chicago area to set up a six-year program; their graduates could, if qualified, enter the university as juniors. A high school at Joliet actually adopted Harper's terminology, and called its "postgraduate" section the Joliet Junior College—the first officially so named.

In the first two decades of the 20th century there appeared some 200 junior colleges, with almost 15,000 students. Some, like Joliet, were attached to conventional high schools; most were private, growing out of business or trade schools (much as college law schools had grown out of private law schools); and quite a few were founded as private college-preparatory institutions. In 1907, California became the first state to set up a system of junior colleges in its high school districts. The plan proved so popular that between 1920 and 1940 the number of junior colleges grew to 575, and the number of students attending them increased to almost 200,000.

As the movement sparked by President Harper spread across the country, Chicago inaugurated another president, Robert Maynard Hutchins, who was alarmed by the domination of the graduate schools and proposed to restore the liberal arts tradition to his university. He combined the last two years of the regular high school with the junior college into a new four-year institution, which he considered ideal for a liberal arts or general education curriculum. In 1942 the revamped College of the University of Chicago began to function according to this plan, and nineteen-year-old B.A.'s, who were as well educated as the twenty-one-year-olds of many conventional liberal arts colleges, sought entrance—not to the junior class in the undergraduate division of the universities—but to the graduate schools. They were received coldly, even at the University of Chicago, whose graduate faculties were in rebellion against the Hutchins plan. And although subsequent studies proved that those students who did gain admission were on the average better Ph.D. material than their peers from other colleges, the experiment crashed against a hostile establishment and was abandoned.

General education is not dead, and the debate continues. On the whole, however, it appears that Harper has triumphed over Hutchins. The junior college has proven enormously successful, and has evolved into the community college—a term intended to accent the relationship of the institution with the local society, as contrasted with the more grandiose and portentous relationship of the university with the greater society. The community college carries on the grassroots services of the land-grant tradition, bringing neighborhood adults up-to-date on a language or a technique and offering a cultural center. This is the part of the system of higher education most likely to succeed as an upward extension of the free public school system. Its Associate in Arts degree takes the stigma off the dropout—a term formerly applied to those who left college prematurely. It does not provide the general education envisioned by the Eliots and the Hutchinses, but neither does it close the academic door to aspiring adolescents.

Hangup on the Campus

Whatever liberal arts may be left in the 20th century must be found on a four-year small college campus. These institutions, which process less than one-third of the college population and send relatively few to graduate schools, may still embody the venerable elitist doctrine formulated by the president of Sarah Lawrence, Esther Raushenbush: " . . . to discover the important questions, to discuss ideas, to explore humanistic studies, not as academic subjects but as ways of being, serves [the] search for a value system as well as for knowledge."

But the private colleges that profess this creed are very few in proportion to the hundreds of institutions offering baccalaureates all over the United States. Most of them draw students partly by default, because they are geographically convenient, or because there is still an attraction to the slower pace or the social life on a small campus. Parents sometimes prefer the aura of chapel and guarded dormitory that has disappeared from other campuses. Alumni send their children. The pious are assured of safe passage for their beliefs at institutions of their faith.

The private four-year colleges are generally expensive, but the state colleges are a good buy for local residents. Neither possess eminent faculties or first-rate libraries or laboratories. A few offer specialties that cannot be matched at any university. A recent development is the "cluster" of several small institutions, each with its own features and its own campus—women's, men's, coeducational liberal arts colleges, a professional school, a graduate center—sharing major facilities and interchanging some curricular offerings. The Associated Colleges at Claremont, California, were the pioneers, and their example has been cited as a possible alternative to the multiversity.

But the community college and the professional institution and the four-year "special-purpose" and liberal arts colleges are all, in the context of modern living, rather limited vehicles of higher education. They provide many more young people than do the schools of any other country with technical or professional skills, many of which will not be used in their actual careers. There is not enough real commitment, in the first undergraduate years, to ensure that a student will stick with the line of work toward which his subject program points. There is likely to be too much specialization in the curriculum to assure a liberal education (one that provides an understanding of one's role in the world), but not enough specialization to profoundly involve the student.

A few years' study of Spanish may prove useful, after graduation, if a position is available with an export firm dealing with Latin America, but it will not of itself impel the graduate to insist on securing such a job; he may find himself buying pulp in eastern Canada and wishing he had taken French instead of Spanish. A chemistry major may be preparing for an expected science opening on a magazine, only to find after graduation that the major developments in the next decade occur in biology. What student could anticipate that a solid background in African culture would virtually ensure a teaching post in the late 1960's?

Nothing in print between hard covers becomes obsolete more quickly than a reference work, just because it is so full of valuable facts. The earth rotates once, and some paragraphs that were true have become lies: the population of Rhubarbia has changed. One encyclopedia refuses to give dates with its data—everything cited occurred "in a recent year." Before many years, even this becomes misrepresentation. This is the fate of much that is taught, because text-books are revised even less frequently than reference works. An archaeological discovery or a medical breakthrough will appear in a scholarly journal and, sometimes, in a news-paper story or a magazine, but years will pass before it is acknowledged officially on campus. The same lag exists in great sequences of information—the researchers do not labor in vain—and the more practical and up-to-date the subject matter seems as it is transcribed from lecture to notebook, the more invalid it is likely to be when (and if) the time comes to use it. This is well known to the academic com-munity, and makes textbook production both an entrenched interest and a lucrative branch of the publication industry. It is hard to avoid the cynical conclusion of Jencks and Riesman:

> . . . the most important thing learned in college may not be physics or history but the importance of credentials and the art of acquiring them.

Undergraduate training does, without question, perform a service for the business and industrial community. It pro-vides much of the skill that once was learned on the job— and not only by apprentices—and the taxpayer or the stu-dent's parents assume the costs. Less obviously, as Jencks and Riesman point out, it has the function of "a kind of protracted aptitude test for measuring certain aspects of both intelligence and character." It separates the boys from the men, in an approximate way, by substituting classroom performance for work performance. Future employers benefit more from the records of grades than do teachers.

In contrast with most of the aspects of undergraduate

higher education just considered, it is possible for both undergraduate and graduate higher education to provide cultural fare of greater and more lasting value. There is not likely to be anything approaching a consensus as to the proper "mix" of liberal (or general) education and vocational (or professional) training desirable, for this is indeed a delicate determination depending on many factors, the most important of which is identification of what is best for the students.

In the early period of the medieval university, when a genuine community of scholars existed—teachers who had recently themselves been students, and students who fairly frequently were intending to teach—conditions favored a cultural regimen beneficial to both. In the United States, when the student population comprises almost half the country's youth, with a variety of backgrounds, personalities, ambitions, and capabilities that would confuse a computer, a neat pattern is not easily worked out. But if such a pattern could be worked out, with the education—not indoctrination or coaching, but education—of young men and women as the primary function, it would surely operate in the universities. The major universities that now dominate all of higher education, however, have other functions, the chief of which is research and development. Moreover, these activities are focused on serving society through its powerful governmental and industrial organs, for which the universities have become specialized annexes.

Consider what has happened to the university in terms of its functions. The original function was to serve as a repository of knowledge and to transmit that knowledge to generations of youth as they arose. This function has steadily been eroded until it is virtually vestigial. A second function, which appeared relatively late in the history of the university in Europe and was transplanted to the United States more than a century ago, was that of advancing the areas of knowledge—in a word, research. This was shortly followed by a third function, indigenous to this country, of purveying knowledge and skills to the community in the best interests of that community—which entails an obligation to ascertain what those best interests might be. The last two functions, research and community service, have become dominant and account for the increasing stress on the vocational (including professional) orientation of the curriculum and on the overpowering importance of the graduate sector. By-products of this trend have been the subordination of undergraduate instruction, the abdication of the faculty from its role in the community of scholars, and above all the growth of an administration-trustee axis in control of university policy.

Educators have long been aware of a "crisis in the universities." Actually, there have been a number of crises. The changeover from the era of elitist grooming to mass education, which is now culminating, was the cause of one crisis. The controversy of vocationalism vs. liberal arts reflected one aspect of this crisis, and has not yet been resolved.

Another crisis—or complex of crises—derives from the imbalance of functions just discussed. For just as the field of mass education advanced beyond the high school to the college level, providing an ever larger and more diverse crop of undergraduates for processing, the plant in which they were to be processed reduced that function to a minimum in order to concentrate on the advancement of knowledge and service to the adult community.

The metaphor above was carefully chosen. Many students who enter the system of higher education feel strongly that they are being processed rather than either trained or educated. An aspect of the multiversity most resented is its resemblance to a think-factory, and although the careers at the far end of the assembly line are relatively assured (as they had never been to previous generations), they lack glamour or even desirability to the more sensitive of the "crop." What is more, the entire society that comprises these careers has become less attractive. No small part of this accrues from the style of the machining, which pervades even the high schools.

As for the advancement of knowledge and the service to the community, these functions formerly had some relationship to the legitimate role of the university. But in past decades they have been utterly perverted. The sector of private enterprise most guilty of widening the gap between rich and poor, and the sectors of government that advance and protect their interests—in short, the components of the military-industrial complex—have adapted to their uses both the research and the service functions of the multiversity to an extent that has become a scandal even among educators. As Harold Taylor, former president of Sarah Lawrence, told a World Affairs Conference:

> The universities have become corporations for producing, transmitting, and marketing knowledge, and in doing so have lost their intellectual and moral identity. At the time that they should have been creative centers for development of strategies for peace, disarmament, and world unity, they were busy with Defense Department contracts. When the educational problems of the Negro were getting worse by the day, they were busy making admission requirements

more and more favorable to the white middle class from privileged environments.

It was not detachment or scholarly perspective that involved the multiversity in this commitment to a controversial policy-making sector of the nation. Nor is it coincidence that the trustees and regents who control the universities have commandeered their facilities on behalf of policies to which they themselves are profoundly committed. Among the enlisted facilities are, of course, personnel from the teaching staff. The abdication of the faculty from participation in the shaping of university policy can be explained only in terms of pragmatism. In the 19th century the rewards, mainly in prestige, shifted from teaching to scholarly research. The second half of the 20th century has seen a further shift; the research is often less scholarly, the rewards are often more tangible. The student, as before, is victimized. John Fischer, who has shown concern as a *Harper's* editor for the victims of the campus crisis, is competent to introduce their case:

> [Students] want to learn something about the world and about themselves—to make an appraisal of their own capacities, and of the dauntingly complex world beyond the campus gates; and to estimate how they might best come to terms with it. . . . What they want is understanding, and they hope to pick up at least a smattering of it by talking to wise, mature men; by reading under these men's guidance; and by observing how such men conduct their own lives. In sum, they are after what used to be called "a liberal education." As recently as twenty years ago they might have found it in most good American universities. Today their chances are close to zero.

CHAPTER SIX

THE CONTEMPORARY
STUDENT MOVEMENT

STUDENT ACTIVITY ON CAMPUS, as we have seen, is not new
in the United States. But both the form and the content
of the activity changed so distinctly, beginning with the first
years of the 20th century, that it is possible to discern the
rise of a student "movement," and this movement has
acquired enough momentum to become a major force in
the contemporary United States and, indeed, in the world.
This had never occurred before, and specialists are now
studying the phenomenon. Many of these studies are, unfortunately, designed to "cope with" or "contain" the impact
of the movement. Some begin with preconceptions based on
emotional bias and seek to explain away the fact that an
increasing number of young people are reacting explosively
rather than to understand whether there is a pattern in
their behavior that might teach society something useful.

What is distinctive about this movement that differen-
tiates it from the relatively sporadic activities of the earlier
student rebellions? These are no mere gripes about butter
that "stinketh" or early curfew or overstrict regimen or
unpopular faculty, although such grievances continue to

appear and may spark a conflagration. The clues must be sought in changes that have occurred within the student population and in the relationships between that population and, one, the campus within which it operates and, two, the entire society of which the campus is a part.

A New Breed

Both the number and the quality of the college student population changed dramatically in the 20th century. The production of high school graduates was just beginning to accelerate at the turn of the century, and in the previous decade college enrollment had doubled. Even so, in 1900 only one out of every 25 persons of college age was seeking a degree and fewer than 30,000 were awarded one. Clearly, there was a vast distinction between the nation's youth and its student population.

Most young men went to work as soon as they could do anything useful, and since most of them were farm boys, there was no break between the hog-feeding after school in their boyhood and the rail-splitting and other more arduous chores befitting young manhood. (No farm boy ever heard of "adolescence.") Those who broke away were more likely to go West than to the cities and least likely to end up on a campus. The campus was, well into the 20th century, the reserve of the privileged young, a cultural hothouse for the slow maturing of special young men and women whose roles in society were assured and desirable.

In a kind of chain reaction, the expansion of the high school population fostered college enrollment; the quest for the bachelor's degree nourished that for the master's and doctor's; and by 1956 more students were enrolled in graduate school than had been in undergraduate school in 1900 — almost a quarter of a million. By this time one-third of the nation's youth was undergoing higher education, obviously no longer an elite. To some extent removed from parental dependence and not yet embarked on a career, a significant number of young people were actually exposed to a kind of experience hitherto reserved for heirs-apparent to a cozy niche in the social structure. They lived in a "make-believe world in which it is 'as if' they were grown up."

Such a world is incompatible with the competitive "real life" for which most of these adolescents were destined. Yet the years of academic life tended to lengthen. By the end of the 1960's, more than 700,000 students were in graduate school, and an increasing proportion of the 6,000,000 hustling for their first degree planned to do postgraduate work. With half of the country's youth on campus, it is not surprising that members of the vast peer group should develop some common traits relating to their common experience, and that among these traits would be a sense of solidarity among themselves.

As Jencks and Riesman comment, earlier generations had challenged particular abuses by their elders. "In the twentieth century, on the other hand, the increasing separatism of teen-age culture and the massing together in high schools and colleges of very large numbers of young people of identical age and social condition have gradually led to a new atmosphere in which the basic legitimacy of adult authority has been increasingly called into question."

This phenomenon of "massing" of youth in educational institutions is one factor that made it possible for "movements" to emerge from situations that otherwise would produce only scattered and impotent episodes of protest. An aspect of "massing" that is particularly meaningful in the present era and that was previously unavailable is that of information. Instantaneous communication has, in effect, forged bonds between the students of scattered campuses in this country and, indeed, throughout the world. Much of the dynamism of the contemporary student (and black) movements can be attributed to electromagnetic waves and jet planes.

No movement operates in a vacuum or captures a sizable segment of a population without the appearance of symptoms that pattern themselves into a syndrome. The laboratory for the incubation of student revolt was, of course, the educational system that allowed its primary educational function to atrophy. The symptoms were the signs of increasing discomfort that pervaded student life until it became a profound malaise. One evidence of this blight was the change in the "style" of student life.

Recall the cocoonlike atmosphere of the colonial period, when academic guardians enveloped their charges (Increase Mather's "children") in a stifling aura of obsolete wisdom. The stirring events of the outside world were muffled, although on occasion an echo penetrated, as a member of the Harvard Corporation revealed in the 1770's:

> The young gentlemen are already taken up with politics. They have caught the spirit of liberty. This has always been encouraged, but they have sometimes been wrought up to such a pitch of enthusiasm that it has been difficult for the Tutors to keep them within bounds. . . .

But, though boys would be boys, the bounds were kept, and it was possible for an undergraduate to admit:

> Amid all the terrors of battle [the Battle of Bunker Hill, nearby] I was so busily engaged in Harvard Library that I never even heard of . . . [it] until it was completed.

The first breaths of fresh air appeared with the student-organized literary societies that sprang up before the Civil War, faintly reflecting the spirit of Jacksonian democracy. At the Free Academy of New York (later to develop into City College):

> During the winter of 1860–1861, with war on the horizon, the literary society, Phrenocosmia, finally debated the issues of secession. The two speakers who upheld it later joined the Confederate Army, while their two opponents served in the Union Army. But the pre-Civil War Phrenocosmians were not touched with the psychology of student movements.

The "young gentlemen" continued to go to college—some of them still abound on small campuses—but as the national pace quickened and the colleges strove to adapt themselves by expanding their curricula and receiving high school graduates, the tone changed. Increasingly, students from lower-middle-class and even working-class families profited from the hospitality of land-grant institutions and saw education as a tool for "bettering" themselves. This type of student, which Kenneth Keniston labeled the "apprentice," flooded the state universities and infiltrated the prestigious seats of learning, accelerating the proliferation of courses, the propagation of departments, in short, the development of the modern university. Like his more aristocratic fellows, he aimed at a career, and although its achievement required drive beyond that expected of the gentleman-in-training, he could be reasonably sure of an honorable and lucrative status in the society into which he would graduate after four years. He had no anxieties; college life could be fun as well as hard work, and there was often time for athletics and fraternal diversions. In fact, Keniston distinguishes another type, the "Big Man on Campus," with the same ambitions as the "apprentice" but different techniques for attaining them. This type substituted personality for hard work to achieve success. "Vocational skills became secondary—or, more precisely, the most important skills in *any* vocation were the capacity to make oneself respected, well liked, and a leader."

Although this type appeared to have some of the capacity to accept leisure and the social graces in the gentlemanly tradition, his drive was as real as that of the "grind." For he, too, was a trainee—an apprentice wheeler-dealer. He flourished in the decades before World War I, then failed to keep pace with the requirement of expertise even in people-handling. His demise was signaled by the appearance of public relations courses in the college curricula.

The future lay with a more streamlined, stripped-down, and souped-up model of the "apprentice," which Keniston terms the "preprofessional." With the same goal as his predecessor—success in the "real world" based upon driving, single-minded effort extended over as many years on campus as necessary—he is an unhappy victim of his own adequacy. He is so *right* for the role of student in the modern university that he has overwhelmed its facilities, overexpanded into its classrooms, compelled it to build, recruit faculty, mortgage itself to industry and government for funds, and open its registers to more and more applicants for a try at higher education. He is, paradoxically, so fit for the multiversity that he has made that institution unfit for him. Meanwhile, the outside world he hopes to grace one day is frantically clamoring for his debut, sending spokesmen of its industrial and military complexes to the campus to solicit his interest. In spite of all this, he appears frustrated.

This seems out of all reason to the generations that matured before World War II, who recall how little a degree meant to employers in the Depression years, and to their children, who strove mightily to achieve a high standard of living in the decade after the war. "What's the matter with those kids?" is their plaintive query. "Everything I had to work for has been given to them. What do they want?" Here is the answer of one student:

> Most of our parents grew up in the Depression, and they were really hurting. They are concerned with money, status, and they're very insecure. Most of us, on the contrary, grew up in the most abundant society the world's ever seen. And to us, abundance isn't something to work for because you have it. You're used to it, it's nothing. So you start getting into human values, because you've gone beyond the security thing. And our parents just can't understand that.

This is absolutely true. Most of the parents can't understand that. The "security thing," for which some of them even picketed and demonstrated as part of the labor movement, and which is symbolized by a trim lawn and a clean car, seems hardly an appropriate target for their heirs presumptive. What values can be more "human" than taking care of your own?

The answer to this may offer a clue as to what happened about the turn of the century to make possible a student movement. Certainly a major factor was the concentration of

youth on campus. Still more important was the fact that
this youth was no longer an elite; American college students were becoming indistinguishable from American youth
in general.

When such a group began to include, for the first time,
a number of individuals who were concerned with human
values transcending their own interests, when a challenge to
the career-oriented student appeared on campus, protest began
to have a new dimension. The new breed lays it on the line:

> . . . any student so dense or just plain selfish that he has
> not perceived the relation between his university education
> and the pressing questions of society has undoubtedly been
> wasting his time.

Activism in the Thirties

An excellent spokesman for the student rebel of the 20th
century was Jack Reed, whose interment in the Kremlin in
1920 proved only that his ten postgraduate years were consistent with his beliefs; he practiced what he preached. He
was an active participant in the then vigorous United States
labor movement, in Pancho Villa's bid for Mexican self-
respect, and in the Bolshevik Revolution (as a reporter he
wrote *Ten Days That Shook the World*). Professor Lewis
Feuer interprets Reed's conduct in terms of "generational
revolt," exemplified by this confession of "guilt":

> All I know is that my happiness is built on the misery of
> other people, that I eat because others go hungry, that I
> am clothed when other people go almost naked through
> the frozen cities in winter; and that fact poisons me, dis-
> turbs my serenity, makes me write propaganda when I would
> rather play.

Another approach toward the Jack Reeds of the world, who form a nucleus of every major student movement, is reflected in a comment by Pope John XXIII: " . . . there are indeed some people who, in their generosity of spirit, burn with a desire to institute wholesale reforms."

The organization that sheltered Jack Reed and a handful of contemporary rebels in the first decade of the 20th century, the Intercollegiate Socialist Society (ISS), was founded in 1905 by a group of nonstudent socialists, a few of whom are still remembered: Jack London, Clarence Darrow, Upton Sinclair. Sinclair, Feuer reports, "was contemptuous of an educational system which had taught him nothing of Kropotkin and Kautsky"—as he well might be. (The charge of educational negligence continued the tradition of those who had sought in the literary societies what their teachers failed to provide, and is extended into the contemporary demand for relevance and particularly for black studies.) The ISS, "the first political student movement in American history," was actually an imported version of study groups that graced many European campuses. Since socialism was a topic of intense interest to contemporaries, the ISS had chapters on 64 American campuses within six years. Virtually none of its members were activists in any sense, although they were busy in the avant-garde lecture circuit and occupied platforms once trod by Emerson and Thoreau, with socialism as the new gospel. Sinclair castigated the educational system in terms that anticipated Clark Kerr: "I have compared Columbia and Minnesota to department stores and Clark and Johns Hopkins to Ford factories. . . . "

When World War I broke out, the ISS met head-on the

challenge to honor *its* preachments: It backed the St. Louis resolution of the Socialist Party and refused to support the war. This stand included direct opposition to military training in 1916, and initiated the continuing campaign against the Reserve Officers Training Corps. After the war, the ISS reappeared as the League for Industrial Democracy (LID), an educational section of the Socialist Party, which reached a pitiable peak of influence in 1920, with almost a million votes for its jailed Presidential candidate, Eugene Victor Debs. When the reformist and revolutionary wings of the Socialist Party were torn apart over the issue of Bolshevism, the LID remained with the former, maintaining the original purpose announced in 1905: "a steady, moderating course in bringing students to a consciousness of the social forces at work in the world today and the role the student must play in society."

The generation that reached the campus immediately after the end of World War I included a number of sharp critics of the war, the peace that was shaping up, and particularly the role of the United States. Much of this was socialist or communist propaganda, but some can be laid at the doors of the colleges, which had been over-eager to participate in war activities. Here is the view reported by a contemporary student, James Wechsler, in *Revolt on the Campus:*

The University of Wisconsin assured the Bureau of Education that "practically all scientific research has been directed into war channels." At the Case School of Applied Science "all courses are taught with more or less of a war view." Yale was even more lavish in its endeavors, providing a new three-year course on subjects relating exclusively to a "military career, as an alternative to the regular college course." . . . The Princeton *Alumni Weekly* boasted that "every day Princeton becomes less an academic college and more a school of war."

So it went, with acceleration of an almost dormant program for military training that was continued after the war had ended and particularly outraged some of the students.

One of the early high points of the anti-ROTC campaign occurred at New York's City College (CCNY) in 1925, when student editor Felix Cohen "reviewed" the corps manual in the campus paper, emphasizing its sections on the techniques of killing. The president of the college ordered Cohen to desist from publishing commentary on the ROTC; the editor left blank spaces to dramatize the censorship and accepted the offer of Heywood Broun for space in the latter's newspaper column. When the president sent Cohen a justification of his position, Cohen refused to publish it on the grounds that it contained forbidden references to ROTC! In a referendum the CCNY students voted overwhelmingly against compulsory ROTC. This was about the most dramatic manifestation of student interest in politics in the 1920's—an era of "normalcy" described thus by Dean Alan Valentine of Swarthmore:

> . . . college and society were teaching [the student] what success was, and the practical ways of gaining it. . . . The quest for personal standing should precede the quest for the welfare of society. All this was in the atmosphere one breathed . . . the college prepared its students for the century they would live in, where one could be successful without ideas and happy without excellence if one accepted majority opinion and got on well with people of one's own kind.

Dean Valentine himself precipitated a minor student flap in 1930 by overriding a student government ruling. He required students to wear coats and ties at lunch and dinner. The students held a mass meeting, passed a resolution condemning the administration for its action, and summoned the president of Swarthmore, the dean, and the chairman of the Board of Managers to hear their objections. The rule was suspended for two weeks, then reimposed, and the student government was asked to enforce the rule. They refused to comply. The student body ignored the rule, and (like the contemporary national law on Prohibition) it remained a dead letter.

This may represent the level of student irritability until the Depression ended all equanimity and forced students, along with other Americans, to question some values they had taken for granted. After economic and social convulsions had shaken the country for a few years, Wechsler, one of the more thoughtful students, who had become something of an "activist" himself, characterized the new breed that was astir on campus:

> They were alert and talented young men and women who had begun to perceive the devastation which economic disorder was bringing not merely to "humanity" . . . but to themselves, as students. That was their premise; from it flowed their conception of the student movement. For, they argued, this was to be no transitory crisis; it was to mark the beginning of the end of the whole system of economic relationships—capitalism. Before it died, that system was to destroy—had already begun to destroy—the "privileged" illusion of the student . . . the vast majority of students, the sons of a sinking middle class, would find themselves steadily propelled into the camp of the dispossessed.

This was the foundation. On the dormant campus of late 1931 it had no horde of followers. But the insurgents proposed that, whether their cohorts accepted this general assumption or not, some structure for unity on specific fronts should be erected. There were immediate local problems—retrenchment, discrimination, the status of academic liberty and opposition to the Reserve Officers Training Corps, on which such joint efforts could be waged. These were to be viewed not as fragmentary, isolated disputes, but as reflections of the external world.

Perhaps even more important . . . was an inquiry into that world. It had been almost forgotten by the campus. . . . The average undergraduate, it must be emphasized, was incredibly ignorant of what was going on beyond his own horizon, of either the nature or complexion of outside society. He boasted of his seclusion. He was snug and lethargic. His curiosity had never been incited, and his educators, as a rule, were content to leave him as he was.

If there was to be a student upsurge, the educative process would have to begin; and that, combined with the intimate hardships of depression soon to be experienced, would demolish complacence. Nothing else would. It was in those terms that the student delegation to Harlan, Kentucky, was conceived.

This "delegation" of some 80 students attempted to publicize the plight of miners who had struck against a wage cut more than a year earlier. Their brutal reception did make some front pages, but to student Wechsler the event signified "the first decisive break with the 'humanitarianism,' condescension and self-sufficiency which had characterized much of the student radicalism of previous years," and he hailed the participants as "an historic vanguard." Lewis Feuer compares this episode with "back-to-the-people" movements of Russian students in 1874, which he had characterized as a "mania" in a class with the tragic and hare-brained Children's Crusade of 1212. Feuer also characterized the action, however, as a "drama of youthful idealism and concern."

There was cause for concern as the bottom fell out of the national economy. The Russian intellectuals of the 1870's, whose careers were guaranteed and who may indeed have been expressing more guilt than empathy in their show of interest in the downtrodden peasants, had never experienced the sense of sickening unease that enveloped American college youth in the 1930's. In the period 1929-34 the number of male college graduates was estimated at between 1,500,000 and 2,000,000. Among these, the percentage of unemployment was placed at between 50 and 85 per cent. Such a situation does not send its victims on quixotic or romantic adventures. It jars them into reality. These young men were brought forcibly to examine social, economic, and political problems that had hitherto been largely outside their range of interests. They began to question the entire fabric of government.

These were questions that the prevailing higher education had not attempted to answer. The thousands of courses that provided information for the solving of specific problems to be faced on the job or in the profession, and the hundreds of courses that professed to summarize and shed light on the wisdom accumulated over the centuries and deposited to the account of this or that discipline, had somehow not included studies of the predicaments facing society in the 1930's.

We teach the ideal conditions of possible worlds passingly fair, but we do not teach the crude conditions of the actual world at all. Thus when we look at what a student learns in the university, we find that it is chiefly confined to what ought to be and is not extended to what actually is.

The competing social and economic systems, for example— communism, fascism, capitalism—had not made the curricular agenda at most universities. Students had not been equipped to respond to what was, on one level, a crisis of intellect. The extent of the crisis may be suggested by a bit of wisdom enshrined in former President Herbert Hoover's Commencement address at Drake University in June, 1935, at the depth of the Depression:

> I hear much lament over the outlook for graduating students. Did it ever occur to you that all the people who now live in these houses, who conduct this vast, complex life and civilization, are going to die? And that just as sure as death, you will take over their jobs?

It is difficult to realize that today's clichés were once startling and brutal statements of incredible plights. We have already accustomed ourselves to the fact that mankind is capable of instantaneous self-destruction, and therefore it is a cliché to make this a point even to justify a sense of discomfort. If sanity is defined as capacity to adjust to reality, then those of us who have adjusted to ultimate or even proximate catastrophe have a right to consider the rest of us as "sick." Earlier revelations—such as the appropriateness of poverty in the midst of plenty—were in similar manner initially staggering, but were eventually adapted into a pattern of acceptability. But in order to understand an earlier generation, it is necessary to strip off some of the accumulated scale, to share the shock of first realization. In the 1930's young people recoiled, not only at the slaughter of pork on the hoof and the pouring of milk into gutters, but also at the prospect of a new war so soon after the recent epic conflict in the name of global democracy. The spread of fascism and nazism, the encouragement of these savage concepts from within the citadels of democracy, the enfeeblement of the League of Nations, the drift toward an unbelievable second world war—these events stirred the youth, on and off campus, in an entirely new way, and gave rise to a vigorous movement whose main thrust was against war and fascism.

The leadership of this movement was assumed by Communists, the designated target of the Axis powers. Their role was facilitated by the permissive attitude taken toward Hitler in the occupation of the Rhineland, toward the Japanese warlords in Manchuria, toward Mussolini in Ethiopia. The sequence of events was later blurred and reduced in significance by the flare of World War II, in which the Blitz and Dresden and Hiroshima muted earlier horrors. Who recalls the Italian airman who poeticized the bombs bursting in the Ethiopian air? Would Guernica have a line in the history books if Picasso had not immortalized this experiment in barbarity? But the slow unrolling of these preludes to disaster shocked American youth.

British students reacted to Hitler's debut in the fellowship of world leaders in 1933 by warning that they would not follow the fascist path toward war. The undergraduates of the Oxford Union voted, 275 to 153, that "this House will not fight for King and country in any war." This was the famous Oxford pledge, and it was repeated throughout the United Kingdom and spread to the United States. In March, 1933, *The Nation* observed:

Conservatives find it difficult to comprehend that American students are extending their interests beyond football, liquor and sex. Even today the average college man does not read a newspaper regularly but the great interest aroused by the peace campaign augurs well for the future. The American college student may be finally emerging from his mental lethargy.

A legendary interlude in the antiwar campaign was provided by President Frederick B. Robinson of CCNY, who made a Canute-like gesture against the tide of restless youth. While the Oxford pledge was on the agenda at campus meetings all over the country, the rebels at CCNY performed their antimilitarist rite by demonstrating against ROTC on May 29, 1933—hallowed by the Establishment as Charter Day but dubbed Jingo Day by the embattled pickets. The president left a tour of inspection to brandish his umbrella petulantly at the demonstrators. Some students deprived him of his weapon, then returned it politely; but Robinson was alarmed. A witness described the aftermath:

> Policemen sit in the shade of the trees on the campus. . . . Faculty members walk rapidly and cringe at their own shadows. It is only the policemen who are self-confident and sure of themselves. It is they who have inherited the college.

In the end, 21 students were expelled and nine suspended for "conduct unbecoming a college student and not in the best interests of the college."

Meanwhile, plans were under way for a wider campaign. The National Student League (NSL; Communist) and the Student League for Industrial Democracy (SLID; mostly Socialist) united their 180 chapters to prepare for a nationwide expression of antimilitarist sentiment.

Only 25,000 students stayed out of class on April 13, 1934, but the action was unprecedented in the history of United States colleges. On some campuses the administration contributed leadership in prayers for peace. At Columbia, following the playing of "Taps" before more than 3,000 in the gymnasium, the chairman commented: "These notes are in memory of those who died in the last war and in solemn declaration that we shall not repeat their mistakes."

Events at Harvard had interesting overtones, in view of subsequent legends concerning the imperturbability of that institution. The student body was sharply divided on the war issue. One group, calling themselves the Michael Mullins Marching and Chowder Club, announced that they would contest the program of the antiwar militants. Wechsler describes the action in Harvard Yard on April 13, 1934:

> By 10:30 groups of students were gathering in front of the Widener steps, scheduled scene of the peace meeting. Their mission was not a solemn one. If there were 200 students in the university genuinely anxious to conduct a protest against war, there were hundreds more who were drawn by no such serious intention. For days there had been reports of the approaching intrusion and Harvard, in its best carnival spirit, prepared for the outing. At exactly eleven o'clock the meeting began. Within three minutes could be heard the oncoming tread of the men of Michael Mullins, who strode on to the grounds with large, flamboyant placards. As they marched in goose-step fashion, they raised their arms in Hitler salutes while the men in front lifted a placard: DOWN WITH PEACE. . . . Then hundreds of residents of Harvard University joined enthusiastically in the show, halting only momentarily to shout final defiance at the outnumbered, hapless sponsors of the

anti-war meeting . . . the troops of Michael Mullins carried the day, successfully averting any possibility of Harvard's alignment with the strike movement.

However, when Harvard alumnus Ernst (Putzy) Hanfstaengl, a member of Hitler's cabinet and composer of the "Horst Wessel" anthem, returned to participate in a Commencement program as a marshal, the administration turned down a suggestion by the Harvard *Crimson* that he be granted an honorary degree.

The antiwar strike of 1935 was even more widespread, bringing out students—for an hour or so—on a large number of scattered campuses, with a total claimed count of 175,000. (At that time some 1,300,000 students were enrolled in the nation's colleges and universities.) By then the two major organizations (SLID and NSL) had merged as the American Student Union (ASU). It was almost entirely the student wing of the Communist Party, and unquestionably a minority faction, but it was able to appeal to the antiwar sentiment of a sizable proportion of the student body on many campuses, and its members were chosen on several of them, including CCNY and Hunter, to lead the official student government organizations.

In the view of the ASU, the democracies of the world, including the United States, were egging on the Axis powers to destroy the Soviet Union. Those who followed the Communist Party position believed, of course, that it was their duty to defend the Communist experiment against any attack; the others merely detested the hypocrisy of the champions of democracy who could support a Pilsudski, a Mussolini, or a Hitler in their anticommunist obsession, and above all who could tolerate the victimization of Ethiopia and China. This two-pronged hostility to war *and* fascism reached a crescendo when, in 1936, a fascist coup in Spain developed into civil war. The democracies once more averted their gaze or mischievously manipulated, but some 3,000 young Americans (perhaps 400 from the campuses), demonstrating that they were by no means all-out pacifists, found their way to Spain to fight for the Republic. About 1,200 were buried there. They were derided as "premature anti-Fascists."

The position of the ASU was ambiguous and untenable during the period of the Nazi-Soviet pact, which its Communist members defended as a stalling action. The organization withered away and had collapsed by the time the United States entered World War II. Fascism had become a deadlier enemy than war, the English students fought for King and country, and students in the United States accepted the call to arms. The student movement had become irrelevant.

Student Government: an Interlude

The generation that appeared on campus in the late 1940's had spent their impressionable years during the Depression and their adolescence during the war. They were aware of the importance of a job; they were the first crop of youth to know that a device had been proven that could extinguish the human race; and they witnessed an intensified use of the repressive power of the state under the supervision of Senator Joseph McCarthy. The idealism that had sparked the late and vain student movement of the 1930's had soured. Among the 2,500,000 students were a sizable contingent of ex-GI's, for whom higher education was a deferred chance to make it, and the college-age youth absorbed some of their big brothers' devotion to cracking the books.

Such a generation found student government a suitable outlet for any vestige of political inclination. As Frances Falvey wrote in 1952, "On most campuses student government is to date the most adequate expression of the belief that students should have a voice in college policy-determination and functioning." And further:

> Student government came into being for a variety of reasons: to rid the faculty and administration of the annoying and time-consuming tasks of discipline; to placate students' demands that their "rights" be recognized; to improve campus morale; to recognize the obvious fact that the college is a cooperative enterprise and that the students are a part of the college with a valuable and necessary contribution to make to the effective functioning of the institution.

The prewar National Student Federation, described by Klopf as "a loosely knit federation of student governments functioning during the thirties, [which] met annually and discussed the organization and principles of student government," could not compete with the ASU in its days of activity. Jencks and Riesman note that:

> Student government is regarded as a charade at most colleges, comparable in intention to the native government established by colonial powers everywhere. It cannot command the respect of the increasingly restless natives because its authority depends entirely on the backing of the "foreign" administration, and the natives therefore want to deal directly with those who have power.

There are other analogies in the labor and civil rights movements. The concepts of company unions and Uncle Toms come to mind. But in the era of the Bomb and Joseph McCarthy, sanctioned student governments had no competition.

One of the legacies of the late war was a convocation of student groups from all over the world, the World Student Congress, which from its first session in Prague in 1946 was clearly inclined toward the political left. The Communist contingents to the subsequently organized International Union of Students (IUS) were well organized and of course subsidized by their governments. The 24 or 25 United States representatives of student governments then convened a national conference of student leaders, which organized the United States National Student Association (NSA).

When it became clear that Communist domination of the IUS was inevitable, the NSA and student delegates from 18 other countries met in Stockholm to form a non- or anti-Communist International Student Conference (ISC), which expanded to a 55-nation student congress by 1950. The NSA strove zealously to marshal the ISC for cold war confrontation with the IUS. Meanwhile, the NSA position on the country's campuses was not really doctrinaire. According to Sol Stern, writing in *Ramparts,* its leaders "moved with the liberal currents of opinion among American students. In the '50s, NSA took even more liberal stands than the prevailing apathy among students might have suggested. And in the '60s, NSA responded to the new militant protest mood on the campuses. It supported students against the draft, opposed the war in Vietnam, and participated in civil rights struggles."

The paradox was clarified by the dramatic revelation in 1967 that the Central Intelligence Agency had been manipulating the NSA since 1952 on the international scene, co-opting or seducing its elected officers systematically, and at the same time providing the financial cushion without which the bastion of student government would doubtless have crumbled like a sand castle. The tolerance or even encouragement of a liberal stance served the double purpose of a red herring and a lollipop. Who would suspect that an outfit stalwartly backing the Student Nonviolent Coordinating Committee could be linked to the CIA? And how could those NSA officers who *knew* of this link have the heart to demolish the undoubted good works of their organization? Some of them, such as NSA director of development Michael Wood (who broke down and told all), "felt horribly trapped in the conflict between their actions and their liberal principles."

After the revelation, NSA was finished internationally, but—having cut its unsavory connections—it tried to make a comeback on campus. It continued its ineffective, mildly liberal advocacy of good causes as a back-up to the new and very powerful competition that had begun to emerge in the 1960's. Representing the official student governments on 300 to 400 campuses, it was out of the mainstream of the movement. This could not be blamed on the CIA— for the NSA never had a chance.

Prelude to Berkeley

It is rather generally accepted that the modern movement dates from the Free Speech Movement (FSM) at Berkeley in 1964. But that historic event and all that followed and continues to follow had a prehistory. Before

FSM there was considerable motion, a supercharged atmosphere, a developing mood compounded of anger and anxiety. It would be simplistic to say that FSM was sparked by the Freedom Rides, and that all these can be traced back to a tired black woman who refused to yield her seat in a bus nine years earlier—or, indeed, to the breaking of the civil rights log jam by the Supreme Court in 1954. But these are the high points along the trail.

In a sense, the judges programmed the movement. They made the first overt move, directing the Southern Establishment to open all its schools to all its citizens, although allowing "deliberate speed" for the process. In her own way, and in the same direction, Mrs. Rosa Parks made her move—or rather, sat tight when she was told to move. Martin Luther King, Jr., interpreted: "The long-repressed feelings of resentment on the part of the Negroes had begun to stir." There had been other such episodes, barely recorded. But this time the combustion was spontaneous; the blacks of Montgomery boycotted the buses—and launched the Southern Christian Leadership Conference (SCLC) and its great leader.

A few years later, four freshmen at the Agricultural and Technical College of North Carolina—one of those minor schools at which blacks could learn a trade—sat at a counter in a five-and-dime store in downtown Greensboro, North Carolina, and waited in vain to be served. One of them recalled: "For about a week we four fellows sat around the A & T campus talking about the integration movement. And we decided we ought to go down to Woolworth's and see what would happen."

Within two weeks, sit-ins had spread to 15 cities in five

Southern states. More than 50,000 people participated during 1961 in some kind of demonstration, and more than 3,000 spent time in jail.

Spontaneous combustion is as natural as fermentation or corrosion. The magnitude of the explosion does not depend on the intensity of the spark, but on the accumulation of combustibles and the restraint preceding the flash. By 1960 the blacks of America were flammable. In this instance, the agents that set them off were students, and this had its repercussions. The organization was born as the Student Nonviolent Coordinating Committee (SNCC). The name soon became a misnomer—few of its field organizers were students, although many of them had been—but an impact had been made: "A Negro never before seen by white Americans was brought into the national view. . . . In early 1960, the Negro student climbed over the wall and into view on millions of television screens all over the country." On TV and in person—the SNCC spokesmen traveled to the campuses seeking aid—black students were seen by white students, and what had begun as a civil rights demonstration became the headwater of a revived student movement. For thousands of these white students went South on the Freedom Rides, learned the techniques of protest along with the rationale of revolt, and brought their messages back with them—notably to Berkeley.

While the NSA was operating its network of student governments and the blacks were building up the steam that would erupt into SCLC and SNCC and CORE (Congress of Racial Equality), another generation was maturing. This generation, 3,000,000 of whom began to appear on campus in the late 1950's, included a leaven of a new kind of radical, described by Paul Jacobs and Saul Landau in *The New Radicals:*

> Many . . . were the children of parents who had been the radicals and left liberals of the thirties and the forties. At home they had heard the discussions about civil rights, and they knew of the political pall that hung over the country during the McCarthy era. They had learned a set of ideals from their parents and now, much to their parents' discomfiture, they were trying to put these ideals into practice. And so by 1960 this new generation was throwing itself against American society, literally and figuratively.
>
> They identified . . . with the Freedom Riders who went South in 1960 and 1961; for this again meant taking direct action with their own bodies against segregation. They were not interested in theory. . . . They felt American society supported racism, oppressive institutions, capital punishment, and wars against popular movements in under-developed countries. "Alienation" was used to describe the society's effects on its citizens, and American society was seen as the source of injustice and suffering everywhere.

Professor Henry May of Berkeley's history department has offered another insight into what he called "a new genre":

> The most striking fact about the present generation, to me, is that large groups are both more idealist and more alienated than any but a handful in the radical thirties. Not only is this student generation critical of the parents and the parental social order; it is often trained to be critical by the parents, themselves perplexed and somewhat guilty in their attitude toward their own times.

Still another aspect appears in the report of an astute editor, A. H. Raskin of *The New York Times:*

> . . . I tried to evaluate the Berkeley uprising against the memories of my own days of rebellion as president of the

C.C.N.Y. class of '31. It was a time when one worker in four was jobless and the misery of the Great Depression was beginning to grip the land. We had been ready to picket our own commencement in cap and gown, but we chickened out at the last minute for fear of losing our degrees. These students . . . were a tougher, smarter breed, more ready to go for broke.

The portrait emerges: idealistic but tough, alienated from society but not ready to abandon it. Certainly apathy had disappeared. David Riesman summarized the dawn of the present movement in an article for the *Atlantic* in 1961, but four years later, when that piece appeared in an anthology, he felt it advisable to comment in a postscript: "Observers who once spoke of students as conformists and apathetic now are worried about them as alienated and assertively disaffected."

Innumerable influences can be cited to explain the changed student of the 1960's. This was the first generation that had never known a time when there was no Bomb, the first for which the end of this planet and voyages beyond this planet were not subjects of science fiction, whose curriculum was trimmed to the specifications of the space age. The cold war ideology seemed absurd, if not indecent, in the light of such events (and in 1962 two world leaders, John F. Kennedy and Nikita S. Khrushchev, seemed to admit as much), but the ideologies that had obsessed the 1930's seemed equally invalid. Dale L. Johnson wrote:

Most of us radicals of the 1960s would agree with Daniel Bell that the postwar years have witnessed the "end of ideology." This we lament rather than applaud. . . . Contemporary "liberalism" is impotent; and no longer even *is* liberalism in our sense. We are tired of the stereotyped responses of the Marxist, and disgusted with the liberal's rhetoric, agnosticism, and incapacity for political action.

In a sense, we are lost, for we do drift about in rough and uncharted seas. Perhaps this is why we have only a dissenting ideology. We unhesitantly express what we are against, but we are less sure of what we are for. . . .

Certainly the bewildered youth found no answers on campus. In California, President Clark Kerr was preparing his statement on "The Uses of the University" for the Godkin Lectures at Harvard, in which he was to point out: "The University is being called upon to educate previously unimagined numbers of students; to respond to the expanding claims of national service; to merge its activities with industry as never before; to adapt to and rechannel new intellectual currents." Then he proceeded to demonstrate that the "national service" (read United States Government and more particularly Defense Department) and "industry" had successfully co-opted this institution; as for the students:

> Recent changes in the American university have done them little good—lower teaching loads for the faculty, larger classes, the use of substitute teachers for the regular faculty, the choice of faculty members based on research accomplishments rather than instructional capacity, the fragmentation of knowledge into endless subdivisions. There is an incipient revolt of undergraduate students against the faculty. . . . It is interesting to watch how a faculty intent on few rules for itself can fashion such a plethora of them for the students. The students also want to be treated as distinct individuals.

It would also be interesting to speculate how the author of this homily could fashion rules that would peculiarly inflame the restless "natives" of the campus—but more on that later.

Perhaps the best spokesman for the student, in describing his sense of being ill-used, is the articulate student himself, such as the anonymous author of a pamphlet entitled "We Want a University":

> As a human being seeking to enrich himself, the student has no place in the Multiversity. Instead he becomes a mercenary, paid off in grades, status, and degrees, all of which can eventually be cashed in for hard currency on the job market. His education is not valued for its enlightenment and the freedom it should enable him to enjoy, but for the amount of money it will enable him to make. Credits for courses are subtly transformed into credit cards. . . .

This sense of being manipulated, of being an item or a digit, is so recurrent that it is perhaps overstressed, or at least not sufficiently related to the very positive response it brought forth: resentment, protest, activism. The "incipient revolt" mentioned by Kerr was already under way.

It took many forms, changing its targets and its style, seldom attacking the university as such, but seizing on one issue or another related to the university, sometimes as a beachhead for a general assault on society. As Jack Weinberg, a former student and an activist, said in an article for a campus paper:

> The University of California is a microcosm in which all the problems of our society are reflected. . . . the individual has lost more and more control over his environment. When he votes, he must choose between two candidates who agree on almost all basic questions. On his job, he has become more and more a cog in a machine,

a part of a master plan in whose formulation he is not consulted and over which he can exert no influence for change. He finds it increasingly more difficult to find meaning in his job or in his life. He grows more cynical. The bureaucratization of the campus is just a reflection of the bureaucratization of American life . . . students are more or less outside society, and in increasing numbers they do not desire to become a part of the society. . . . The students, in their idealism, are confronted with a world which is a complete mess, a world which in their eyes preceding generations have botched up. . . . They affirm themselves; they decide that even if they do not know how to save the world, even if they have no magic formula, they must let their voice be heard. They become activists. . . .

It was in this mood that the Free Speech Movement was initiated at Berkeley.

In 1957 a group proposing to run a slate of candidates for the student government organization (Associated Students of the University of California, or ASUC) adopted the name of SLATE. Already involved on a small scale in civil liberties and against the ROTC, SLATE added new planks to its platform for 1958, including one against discrimination in the fraternities and another concerning rents for students—nothing spectacular, but they won two seats in ASUC. Then the new administration of President Clark Kerr kicked the ball, and the contest was on.

A limitation on students' "off-campus" activities was announced, presumably to conform to a legal requirement imposed on the university as a state unit. A code, known as Kerr's Directives, was proclaimed on October 23, 1959. As the interest in "off-campus" activities increased, these directives chafed until they became intolerable. One activity

in 1960 was the campaign against the House Committee on
Un-American Activities (HUAC); students were hostile
spectators at the committee's hearings in San Francisco, and
hundreds were washed by firehoses down the steps of City
Hall. Students responded enthusiastically to SNCC's sit-in
campaign by picketing dime stores in Berkeley, and 180
were arrested. Many of these activities, and some more
remote in scope—such as support for the Cuban revolution,
then in its early phase—required financing. The dispersal of
leaflets and the collection of funds were blocked by the
Kerr Directives. Protests now arose against these ukases—
in the *Daily Cal,* for example:

> In a democratic society, the source of authority for such
> regulations is rightfully derived from the society's con-
> stituents, which in the case of a student community are
> the students and not the university administration.

ASUC voted, 11 to 4 (the 4 were all SLATE), to support
the Kerr Directives. However, ASUC also conducted a
survey of 20 schools with large student bodies and found
that in 16 of them student government organizations were
still permitted to take positions on off-campus matters.

The tempo of activity increased in 1963 and 1964. The
main motif was civil rights, the principal target was discriminatory practice, and the largest demonstration was that
at the Sheraton-Palace Hotel in March, 1964, involving
hundreds of students. But the level was relatively moderate
throughout: ". . . at least until the Free Speech Movement of 1964, both sides showed great patience, a willing-
ness to adhere to the rules, and a conviction that ultimately victory would go to the side with the better reasons."

This reasonable procedure, and its accomplishments, can

be traced with some precision in the case of ROTC at Berkeley. In an unapproved poll on campus in 1934 in which 1,200 students took part, the vote was two to one against compulsory ROTC. ASUC requested President Sproul in vain to adopt a voluntary program. In 1956, ASUC itself conducted a poll; again voluntary ROTC was favored; this time the request for change went to the Regents, who sat on it until the end of 1960, when they decided to do nothing. In May, 1962, President Kerr raised the question once more, and in June the Regents voted to make ROTC voluntary. Considerable picketing by SLATE may or may not have influenced the decision.

It must be emphasized that the students did not, at this time, direct much of their hostility toward the campus. The Kerr Directives, however, were obstacles to the effective realization of their off-campus goals, and marginally affected the activists. SLATE, in an effort to revise "the uneasy balance of administrative powers and student rights, . . . suggested that policy-making power in the university be transferred from the Regents and the administration to the faculty and the students. The university treated the proposal lightly." Nevertheless, it was a "last straw" of administrative display of power that was to set off the outbreak in the fall of 1964, known as the Free Speech Movement, the repercussions of which continue to agitate the nation's campuses.

Free Speech for Openers

The event that precipitated the Berkeley student revolt of 1964 was a letter of September 14 from the dean of students to all student organizations banning certain activities related to off-campus causes in a specific area belonging to the university in which such activities had been tolerated for some time—although this toleration conflicted with the Kerr Directives. This letter was analogous to the strict enforcement of the Navigation Acts by the British in the 1770's—George III could insist that these acts had all along been on the books, and the chancellor at Berkeley could declare (as he did on October 1): "No instance of a newly imposed restriction or curtailment of freedom of speech on campus can be truthfully alleged. . . ." But the students reacted vehemently, 18 of their organizations forming a United Front that was to name itself, early in October, the FSM. All of them, including Conservative and Republican clubs (which soon detached themselves from the movement) defiantly set up tables, distributed literature, and solicited funds in the prohibited zone.

Then the administration committed its "Intolerable Acts" comparable to those of Parliament against Boston in 1774 to retaliate for the Tea Party. A dean picked out five leaders among the hundreds who were challenging the edict and ordered them to appear for disciplinary action. When a petition signed by more than 500 students, who declared their equal guilt, was brought to the administration, three of the petition-bearers were added to the candidates for punishment. The penalty, after the eight selectees refused to appear for their sentence, was indefinite suspension.

It later turned out that university regulations made no provision for any discipline without hearings, and that indefinite suspension was not one of the penalties listed in the regulations. A faculty committee eventually concluded:

"We were left with the impression that some or all of these eight students were gratuitously singled out for heavy penalties summarily imposed in the hope that by making examples of these students, the University could end the sit-in and perhaps forestall further mass demonstrations."

The "sit-in" referred to was an impromptu gathering of the petition-signers in the halls outside the chancellor's office, part of the effort to assure equality of treatment for all protesters. The next day, October 1, the forbidden tables were again set up—now in Sproul Plaza, between the student union and the administration building (Sproul Hall). This time the administration escalated the action by attempting to arrest Jack Weinberg, who presided at the CORE table.

Weinberg had time, before sufficient force could be marshaled, to tell a throng of students gathering around him in Sproul Plaza:

> We want to see social change in the world in which we live. . . . We think, we talk, we discuss, and when we're done thinking and talking and discussing, well then, we feel that these things are vacuous unless we then act on the principles that we think, talk, and discuss about. This is as much a part of a university education as anything else.
>
> We feel that we, as human beings first and students second, must take our stand on every vital issue which faces this nation, and in particular the vital issues of discrimination, of segregation, of poverty, of unemployment; the vital issue of people who aren't getting the decent breaks that they as individuals deserve. . . .

At that moment the police car reached the center of the plaza, and immediately the veterans of the campaigns in

Mississippi set their bodies on the ground before and behind the car and, once Weinberg was inside, all around it.
For 32 hours the car was thus surrounded by experts at
organized nonviolence. From the top of the besieged vehicle
orators harangued the students (who swelled to about 4,000
by noon of October 2), pro and con, radical and moderate,
other students and faculty members, and even a priest, who
succeeded in quieting some hecklers. Messages were relayed
to the administration, almost 1,000 police were deployed
in Sproul Hall, and the university had become the scene of
a full-fledged student revolt.

Finally, in the evening of October 2, a truce was signed
between the student representatives and the administration, and within minutes its contents were read from the
top of the police car. The question of the appropriate discipline for "the eight" was to be discussed by a faculty
committee; other major policy questions in dispute were to
be discussed by a joint student-faculty-administration committee; and the students could feel that they had made at
least some impression. Their spokesman, Mario Savio,
said: "Let us agree by acclamation to accept this document.
I ask you to rise quietly and with dignity and go home."
This was done.

During the next weeks much activity took place. The
FSM was organized. It was discovered that the faculty committee assigned to determine appropriate discipline for the
suspended students did not exist. President Kerr proposed
to substitute an appointed committee; he finally agreed to
let the faculty select a committee that would be purely
advisory. Similarly, the committee on policy turned out to
consist of ten Kerr appointees and two from the FSM—

a setup that the FSM rejected outright. By mid-October
an impasse had been reached, and for almost two months
the administration tried to whittle away its concessions of
October 2.

The situation deteriorated rapidly. The Regents responded
to a request for a meeting with FSM by stating that "no
useful purpose would be served by considering whether your
group should be heard by the Regents at this time
[October 15]." The chancellor rejected a request by the
faculty committee on discipline to reinstate "the eight."
The tripartite committee on policy, which had been expanded so that only 12 of the 18 members would be Kerr
appointees, and which had been accepted by the FSM, was
bogged down on precisely what off-campus causes could
be promoted on campus.

The FSM lost patience and again set up tables on Sproul
Plaza on November 9, whereupon Kerr dissolved the committee. On November 20 the Regents met, while about
5,000 students awaited their decision in Sproul Plaza. The
Regents grandly ignored the recommendations on discipline
by the faculty committee and the recommendations on
policy by the dissolved tripartite committee. The rules on
campus activity were liberalized in an ambiguous way, but
a roster of disciplinary cases was compiled for further consideration, and procedures for both discipline and enforcement were tightened. In sum, a minimum of the points
raised in the protest were conceded, but those who raised
the points were penalized, and further protest was virtually
banned.

The predictable result, of course, was further protest. A
rally on the plaza heard an FSM spokesman, Weinberg, tell
the administration:

Listen to my voice; you haven't heard me before; you ignore me. I came out in 5,000, and you didn't recognize me. You didn't even mention me. I sent in petitions; you didn't read them. I put forward platforms; you didn't study them. You cannot ignore me any longer; and I'm going to put myself in a position where I cannot be ignored, because you're going to have to look at me.

Then a few hundred sat in at Sproul Hall for a few hours and went home.

The movement was clearly fatigued and almost out of steam. But the administration primed it by announcing, on November 28, the expulsion of four student leaders for their activities *after* the October 2 agreement—which was supposed to have led to an armistice. Most of the students and some of the faculty were outraged. According to a pro-FSM historian, this single act was "to sweep up the support of a clear majority of the campus for the first time. . . ."

The FSM made a last attempt to reach the administration, demanding an end to persecution and "immediate and substantial improvements" in the rules, adding: "We have published our platform, asked for public discussion, petitioned, sent delegations, demonstrated, held a moral protest. Yesterday we demanded, and now we await a reply." Failing this, they promised "massive direct action."

The plea unanswered, some 6,000 gathered on campus on December 2 to hear Mario Savio make a statement that has been quoted innumerable times, and that somehow lacks the air of intransigence conveyed by portions of it taken out of context. In response to a "liberal" who pointed out that Kerr could no more act contrary to the wishes of the Regents than a company manager could flout his board of directors, Savio responded:

. . . if this is a firm, and if the Board of Regents are the
Board of Directors, and if President Kerr is in fact the
manager, . . . then the faculty are a bunch of employees
and we're the raw material. But . . . we're human beings.
. . . There's a time when the operation of the machine
becomes so odious, makes you so sick at heart, that you
can't take part. And you've got to put your bodies upon
the gears and upon the wheels, upon the levers, upon all
the apparatus, and you've got to make it stop. And you've
got to indicate to the people who run it, to the people
who own it, that unless you're free, the machine will be
prevented from working at all.

Then almost 1,000 students occupied Sproul Hall. The
technique of the sit-in had been perfected in the 1930's by
labor, and its use had been adapted as a major form of
nonviolence by the civil rights movement in the early 1960's.
College facilities had been occupied before—for example, in
1936, when the ASU-led students took a hall at City College to demonstrate against the firing of a Communist professor. There had been a sit-in at the University of Chicago
earlier in 1964, which had petered out after nine days. But
in a sense this was the ultimate weapon of the aroused
students, and although it had been used tentatively twice
before at Berkeley, it was not used lightly.

Kerr would have preferred to follow the Chicago tactic of
ignoring it, according to Hal Draper, but Governor Edmund Brown called for the strong arm of the law. More
than 600 police took more than 12 hours to clear the
building, and every one of the culprits was incarcerated
pending the arrival of bail. This guaranteed the success of
the student strike that had been called to support the sit-in.
The ASUC deplored the situation, condemned the sit-in

and strike, and prophesied disaster for the university, looking nervously toward Sacramento. Organized alumni registered their disapproval. But the strike stuck—the "machine" ceased to function.

The administration attempted a coup of the sort that enraged student opinion. One day before the scheduled meeting of the Academic Senate (the faculty "legislature"), the chiefs of the departments met and produced a "solution," which President Kerr announced at a vast convocation. The strike was declared ended, and the administration agreed to accept the courts' penalty against the arrested students and abstain from imposing any further discipline. The floor was refused to Savio, who then tried to seize the microphone; after he was physically dragged from the stage, the chairman was persuaded to let him speak—and he merely announced a rally to take place immediately on the plaza: "Please leave here. Clear this disastrous scene, and get down to discussing the issues." The rally, attended by almost 10,000, heard one student point out: "The sit-in did not obstruct, but rather caused, the first rational discussion of the problem on this campus." The strike continued.

The next day, December 8, saw the final triumph of the FSM. In elections for vacancies on ASUC, FSM candidates were chosen for all seven openings—a striking mark of student approval. The major interest, however, was on the Academic Senate, which held a full-length debate on the issues. With the largest attendance of that body yet recorded, and with thousands of students following the reasoning of their teachers over a public address system, the faculty voted, 824 to 115, against any university disciplinary measures against students for activities to date;

to accept the FSM interpretation of the rules for political activity on campus; and to assure that future disciplinary matters would be the concern of the faculty. Overjoyed at this support, FSM issued a statement:

> With deep gratitude the Free Speech Movement greets the action of the faculty. . . . Now that the University community is again united, we hope it will work together for speedy implementation of its proposals. . . . We regret having been forced to undertake controversial action to begin a dialogue. The actions have weighed more heavily on us than upon any others in the academic community. We hope that the dialogue which has at last begun will mean that such actions will never again be necessary.

From Kerr, no comment pending the scheduled meeting of the Regents—as was suitable to the "manager" of the firm. As might have been anticipated, the Regents rejected the proposal of the Academic Senate and chose to "direct the administration to preserve law and order"; to "reconfirm that ultimate authority for discipline . . . is constitutionally vested in the Regents, and is a matter not subject to negotiation"; to undertake to review campus rules themselves and, pending any changes, to enforce existing rules.

The bark was fierce, but the FSM retained shreds of victory. Chancellor Edward Strong was retired ("for health reasons") and his successor, Martin Meyerson, acceded to most of the actual student demands in practice. Sproul Plaza was the scene of busy tables for sundry causes and, on January 4, 1965, of its first legal rally.

Then the FSM disintegrated. Its components—CORE, Students for a Democratic Society (SDS), and the others—were now in a position to function effectively (which is what the FSM was all about in the first place), and proceeded to do so.

Study War No More

Civil rights continued to arouse the interest of students in 1965, but their greatest concern developed over the intensification of the United States' participation in the war in South Vietnam. As the number of American combatants increased during that year from 20,000 to 190,000, such questions as the draft, ROTC on campus, university involvement in war planning and waging, and United States foreign policy were no longer abstract subjects to the students or, for that matter, to the faculties. A national debate on the American role in Vietnam began in the spring of 1965, and naturally the students and teachers were among the most vocal.

In March a group of 49 faculty members at the University of Michigan issued a call for a "work moratorium" to discuss the issues. The action is described in *Teach-ins: U.S.A.*, edited by Louis Menashe and Ronald Radosh. It was very appropriately designated a "teach-in," but in view of the experience of Berkeley, there was concern "that the Vietnam issue was about to be completely submerged in the ensuing fight about the legality, the ethics, the prudence, and the effectiveness of a work moratorium" and that a "debate on the 'nature of academic freedom' was about to erupt and to drain the rhetorical energies of the university community." So it was agreed to "shift from regular working hours to night hours . . . to undercut all the talk about 'breach of contract,' 'propaganda in the classroom,' 'infringing on the right of the taxpayers,' 'depriving the students,' and so on."

It was agreed that the protesters should make it clear that the United States, not the university, was the target. The university cooperated, providing auditoriums and classrooms. As a kind of bonus, the project "established a genuine rapport between students and a segment of the faculty . . . and effected a fusion of scholarly analysis and deep personal concern." At the end of one teach-in, a student rose and said, "I'm just a lowly freshman, but this teach-in shows me what a university has to be."

The technique spread from campus to campus and received wide publicity. Two months later, a national teach-in was organized. But by this time the professors on both sides of the debate had taken over. Some regretted the slighting of the students: "The reactions that meant the most to me were those of students who, afterward, claimed that the teach-in was the most meaningful *educational* experience they had ever had."

A graduate student wrote: ". . . they could not learn this without their students. For, if the radical potential of campus teach-ins is to be realized, discussions, decision, and action cannot take place at faculty meetings, but must take place in the classrooms, where the teach-in began."

Having become formalized as a debate, the teach-in was virtually domesticated, kept within bounds; the issues were talked to death—although much was aired that would prove useful by the time another 30,000 young Americans had lost their lives in Southeast Asia.

Alongside the teach-ins, the students began to adopt other traditional techniques of protest. The events at Berkeley well illustrate the process on many campuses.

Steve Weissman of the FSM and others organized the

Vietnam Day Committee, which joined with similar groups elsewhere to form a loose alliance for conducting peace demonstrations. A massive turnout in mid-October, 1965, involved protesters in about 40 cities, including the Bay Area; about 10,000 marched from Berkeley to Oakland, where they were stopped by city police. However, a month later, the seven-mile march was completed, under the protection of the National Guard. An attempt to block the movement of troop trains in the Bay Area resulted in the arrest of four activists in August.

The free-speech question was refought at Berkeley in 1966 in the context of the war. Students and nonstudents on November 30 set up an antiwar table on campus to compete with the Navy recruiting table. The administration allowed the Navy to carry on but declared the peace tables contrary to regulations. In the end the police were called in, and "nonstudent" Mario Savio was one of those arrested. Savio had been the most severely penalized of the students found guilty for the 1964 events, the university having refused to readmit him.

Almost all student organizations supported the strike that followed the arrests of 1966. But the chancellor refused to negotiate, declaring that this was a "struggle for power"—with the existence of the university at stake. This time the faculty supported the administration, 795 to 28, and the strike was called off. Savio was convicted and sentenced to another 90 days in jail and fined $350. Nevertheless, in October, 1967, Berkeley students held a forbidden antidraft rally on campus, and when this resulted in the suspension of two students, a "mill-in" closed Sproul Hall for two days in November.

As the intensity of the war increased, so did the hostility toward it on campus. However, there were student expressions of support for the national policy at Michigan State, Rutgers, University of Rhode Island, and elsewhere. Philip Sherburne, president of the NSA, affirmed that students accepted the United States presence in Vietnam but hoped the war would soon be brought to an end. (This was before exposure of the NSA-CIA link.) The SDS at first announced it would help conscientious objectors keep out of the armed services, but after a referendum in 1965 showed that 56 per cent of its members disapproved of this line, it proposed alternative service for objectors. In November the SDS participated in a peace march to Washington. Administration spokesmen—Dean Rusk, Robert McNamara, Arthur Goldberg, Hubert Humphrey—were rudely greeted by pickets and members of student audiences. The opposition included pacifists who opposed all wars, radicals who believed this war was immoral or unjustified or both, and a few who held that right was on the side of the "enemy." A Rutgers professor who dared espouse the last position was supported by some students and, in proof that the era of crude suppression was over, was able to remain on the faculty.

By 1968 it was so obvious that the war had become an "overriding concern" to students that the following statement appeared in the Cox Commission Report on the April outbreak at Columbia:

> The University became the focus of both criticism and frustration whenever it could be linked with the defense establishment; in furnishing class rankings to draft boards, in making facilities available for ROTC programs, in per-

mitting recruitment for the Armed Forces or war-related industries, and in government research. . . . On the war, therefore, even more than on other issues, the university becomes a surrogate for society. . . .

The report acknowledged that many large universities, among them Wisconsin, Michigan, and Harvard, had experienced major demonstrations against their "alleged complicity" in the war in Vietnam. The report then reviewed events at Columbia: the blocking of naval ROTC participants in a ceremony from entering Low Library, May, 1965 (resulting in the first call-up of city police on that campus); an SDS-organized interference with CIA recruitment, November, 1966; a sit-in to prevent CIA interviews (Columbia's first sit-in), February, 1967; a mill-in to interfere with Marine Corps recruitment, April, 1967; an SDS-sponsored picket line followed by a demonstration inside Dodge Hall to protest recruitment by Dow Chemical, February 28, 1968; an SDS-led demonstration into Low Library to protest university affiliation with the Institute for Defense Analyses (about which more below), March 27, 1968.

At Columbia, SDS leader Mark Rudd declared in a manifesto in October, 1967: "Let us clearly state that our goal is to end university complicity with the war: IDA, NROTC, CIA contracts, recruiting, etc." It was as simple as that—and on a large number of campuses.

Harassment of recruiters—whether for the uniformed or the corporate sector of the military-industrial complex—was something rather new. Columbia's first challenge to war recruiting on campus, on November 15, 1966, preceded that at Berkeley by two weeks and was directed against CIA rather than armed forces agents. But it was the SDS attempt to obstruct Marine recruitment in April, 1967, that induced some features of the Columbia action of 1968 very like those at Berkeley four years earlier.

The opposition to the Marines at Columbia produced a reaction against the SDS that was reflected in a referendum on campus, in which 67 per cent of those voting supported the idea of open recruiting. The administration, however, refused to ride with the victory. President Grayson Kirk had appointed a faculty committee "On Student Life" to consider rules. The committee reported back after two years, in August, 1967, with a "unanimous recommendation for the adoption of new and detailed regulations defining the permissible limits of indoor demonstrations. . . ." No action was taken on this or other portions of the report. Instead, the president, on September 25, 1967, issued a statement of policy containing a blanket prohibition: "Picketing or demonstrations may not be conducted within any University building."

Thus what may be called the "Kirk Directives" presented Columbia with its version of the free-speech issue. As at Berkeley, the other substantive issues, including those related to the war, became secondary to the need to repel the presidential offensive. The administration tried to ignore or explain away a series of deliberate violations, but it was such a violation that was to precipitate the April, 1968, outbreak.

The issue chosen for this violation was Columbia's participation in the war effort. This also had a prehistory. After the nation had learned of the link between the NSA and the CIA, radicals began a hunt for further ties. Columbia SDS reported, later in 1967, a discovery that the CIA had been funding a Columbia research project on the economies of East Central European countries. At first Kirk and also Andrew Cordier (then a dean and perhaps ignorant of the source of the funds for a time) denied the story; but when Cordier began to unravel the ties (just as did NSA), it was apparent not only that the SDS report was grounded in fact, but that the administration had been less than frank.

After SDS showed that a kind of "transmission belt" between Columbia and the Pentagon, called Electronics Research Laboratories, had been involved in secret research on ballistic missiles to the tune of several million dollars, the laboratory severed its organizational ties with Columbia and was renamed the Riverside Research Institute, although its directors and faculty still interlocked with Columbia's. After SDS established that Military Intelligence was working out of Columbia, the university terminated the agreement. Then SDS began its offensive against the Institute for Defense Analyses (IDA), and the university reacted predictably.

The IDA had been established by the Department of Defense and Joint Chiefs of Staff in 1955 in a move to obtain university research and advice upon military matters. Columbia had affiliated in 1959, and by 1968 it was one of a dozen institutions of higher learning that held IDA membership. None of this was secret. It had merely become monstrous, in the view of many students, in the context of the war in Vietnam, just as had ROTC and the draft. At many of the participating universities, hostility to IDA was aired; at Columbia, 1,500 student and faculty signatures were gathered on a petition for disaffiliation. The trustees responded by confirming support for the IDA but offered to substitute the personal membership of university officials on the IDA board in place of institutional membership. This proposal further angered some critics, who saw it as an effort to end the relationship in form but not in substance. This tactic, in short, became the basis of one of the demands in the April revolt.

In the end, the IDA itself adopted, as policy, the very tactic proposed by the Columbia trustees—it ended all institutional affiliations. Thus the protesting students helped foil one attempt to enmesh their institutions (along with part of the faculties), and clarified the role of both the trustees and the students.

The day before the Columbia protest entered its active phase, a professor of physics from Haverford College, attending a convention in New York, was quoted by a reporter as saying that "the climate on American campuses was such that the United States could not now organize a major military research effort such as the Manhattan Project." Other physicists cited actions by Cornell, Pennsylvania, Michigan, Chicago, and California universities and the Massachusetts Institute of Technology as proof that secrecy was being rejected by the colleges. All classified research had already been rejected by the University of Pennsylvania. (A year later MIT was to declare a moratorium on such research—and MIT was the institution most favored by Federal grants and particularly by defense grants, amounting to $96 million and $47 million respectively in 1967.) As *New York Times* reporter Evert Clark summed up the views of the antiwar Federation of American Scientists, "The basic argument offered against secret research on the campus is that it directly opposes the generation and free dissemination of knowledge that a university is supposed to promote."

Some teachers were catching up with the students. But somehow the students always managed to stay just in advance of their elders. An instance occurred at Stanford University, whose trustees were responsible for appointing the board of the affiliated Stanford Research Institute. Founded in 1946, the institute engaged in research largely useful to the military, and it was the target of a student protest in the spring of 1969 that culminated in the occupation of an administration building. The students were soon evicted by the police, but the trustees got the message and two weeks later voted to put the institute up for sale. The students, noting that the IDA did not cease to function on behalf of war as soon as its formal ties with the universities had been loosened, altered their demand. They did not want the university to sell the institute so that it might continue its research in chemical and biological warfare (CBW) and counterinsurgency; they wanted the university to retain the institute and to convert it into a service institution on behalf of the community.

The result was a compromise—the purchasers might continue the counterinsurgency (but not the CBW) program, but must also engage in programs relating to the solution of social problems.

The campaign against ROTC was perennial, certain to appear on any campus that afforded its facilities to the military. Long before the war in Vietnam, students had asserted that an institution of higher learning was not an appropriate place to learn the arts of war. It was inevitable, however, that the conflict in Vietnam should sharpen the struggle against ROTC, that the survival of ROTC on campus should be eroded, and that the Defense Department should attempt to accommodate itself to the trend.

Between 1964 and 1969, about 40 campuses dropped compulsory ROTC, and in the first half of 1969 the academic standing of the war-training courses declined at such prestigious institutions as Yale, Harvard, Dartmouth, Cornell, and Brown.

Some students were not satisfied with what they considered halfway measures, and they demanded immediate and complete termination of all armed forces training on the campus. The Harvard SDS led an occupation of University Hall in April, 1969, mainly to urge the administration to break all existing ROTC contracts instead of following the faculty decision to end the academic status of the military curriculum. President Nathan Pusey surprised the students by using force immediately, and a number of heads were clubbed; a stern judge meted out 169 fines. As at Columbia, the moderates then sided with the radicals, not because they hated "Rotcy" so much as because they condemned Pusey's recourse to violence. The united student front survived only a week's strike. The Corporation backed Pusey and stated that abolition of ROTC "would constitute an indefensible breach of faith with the students now enrolled."

In May, 1969, 45 Dartmouth students went to jail after police dislodged them from an administration building, where they had holed up in a similar anti-ROTC demonstration.

Columbia became the first major university to accept a total break with a military training program already well established, although its trustees agreed, in mid-May, 1969, to phase ROTC out over a two-year period. While unwilling to admit that the students' 1968 demands had played any part in bringing about the decision, Acting President Cordier did say that the program might be considered inappropriate because it was "operated by an outside agency." The discovery would seem belated, and its logic, if applied consistently, could be extended to support virtually all student objections, not only to ROTC, but also to most recruitment on campus.

Black and White

The increasing concern on campus with the war in Vietnam and related issues did not by any means overshadow the involvement of students in the campaign for civil rights. As that campaign accelerated to keep pace with the trend toward passage of civil rights acts (beginning in 1964), it changed its character, its tactics, and even its strategy. These changes in turn affected the participation of students.

Civil rights are not favors to be "granted" to blacks through legislation. Their constitutional existence had been confirmed in some instances by specific legislation and by court decisions, but their practice had not been consistently enforced. The civil rights activists in the early 1960's intended to spotlight this situation, to arouse public opinion, and to compel enforcement. This had been the motive behind the lunch-counter sit-ins in 1960, organized by students, and the Freedom Rides in 1961, in which black and white students participated.

As the Presidential election year of 1964 approached, special emphasis was given to efforts to get blacks to register and vote, so that they could exercise their legitimate

political power, especially in the South, where their numbers might become decisive. Casualties suffered in this
campaign included the three martyred volunteers, one black
and two white, who were murdered in Neshoba County,
Mississippi, in June, 1964. Out of this struggle came the
black-and-white Mississippi Freedom Democratic Party,
whose delegate dramatically challenged the national Democratic Party convention in 1964 to restore democracy to
their state. The official rejection of this bid, by the party
that posed as the champion of civil rights, contributed to
the frustration of the blacks and convinced many of them
that success in politics would no more solve their crucial
problems of decent survival in white America than the
Supreme Court decision of 1954 had placed their children
in white schools.

Other events in 1965 and 1966 sharpened this frustration.
The march from Selma to Montgomery seemed to advance
the cause, inasmuch as President Lyndon Johnson also
promised to "overcome," and the Congress passed another
civil rights act. But a bitter aftertaste prevailed. Federal
forces had efficiently shepherded the official march, but they
did not prevent the murders of a Boston clergyman and a
Detroit housewife. Such treatment of white friends convinced many blacks that they would have to win their own
freedom in their own way. When it took a United States
Supreme Court decision to force the Georgia legislature
to seat Julian Bond, a black leader of SNCC, after three
electoral victories, the ballot box lost some of its mystique.
When James Meredith—who had been thrust into the University of Mississippi by Federal force against state force—
tried to prove that a black man could walk the highways

of his state unmolested, and was promptly shot from ambush, the slogan of Black Power took hold and split the
black civil rights movement.

The organizations that had most welcomed student participation (SNCC and CORE) decided to depend no longer
on white support. The mood was not one of hostility to
all whites or rejection of white assistance. Events had merely
shown that the dream of assimilation of the long-rejected
blacks into the white American community—"integration"—
could never be realized by appeals to brotherhood, love, or
the United States Constitution. A handful of well-intentioned
white allies could not secure for blacks as individuals the
privileges of full citizenship—blacks would have to win
these for themselves, and (as some of them phrased it) by
"any means necessary." This doomed integration as an
immediate goal. A manifesto issued by SNCC members in
Atlanta in 1966 presented the new mood:

> There is no doubt in our minds that some whites are just
> as disgusted with this system as we are. But it is mean-
> ingless to talk about coalition if there is no one to align
> ourselves with, because of the lack of organization in the
> white communities. There can be no talk of "hooking-up"
> unless Black people organize Blacks and white people
> organize whites. If these conditions are met, then perhaps
> at some later date—and if we are going in the same direc-
> tion—talks about exchange of personnel, coalition, and other
> meaningful alliances can be discussed.

In this same manifesto, the role of the participants in the
recent civil rights actions, mainly students, was considered
without rancor:

This is not to say that whites have not had an important role in the Movement. In the case of Mississippi, their role was very key in that they helped give Blacks the right to organize, the right to picket, the right to demonstrate, the right to print. . . . Since these goals have now been accomplished, their (whites') role in the Movement has now ended. What does it mean if Black people, once having the right to organize, are not allowed to organize themselves? It means Blacks' ideas about inferiority are being reinforced. Shouldn't people be able to organize themselves? Blacks should be given this right. Further [white participation] means in the eyes of the Black community that whites are the "brains" behind the Movement and Blacks cannot function without whites. This only serves to perpetuate existing attitudes within the existing society. . . .

Within this statement, and soon to be made very explicit, were not only the rationale behind Black Power, but also the elements of the "Black-is-Beautiful" concept: "Organizing must be done by Black people who are able to see the beauty of themselves, are able to see the important cultural contributions of Afro-Americans. . . ."

Black on Black

The major role in the new phase of the struggle for civil rights on campus naturally fell to the black students. They were, indeed, a minority of a minority—for the proportion of black youth who would ever reach college was minute in 1966, at a time when the proportion of white youth was increasing spectacularly. (This had important side effects: student deferment from the draft, for example, heavily favored white youth.)

Most blacks on the campus were in the network of Negro

colleges that had been permitted to survive for the express purpose of training a corps of black intellectuals to serve the black community—or to provide token upper-echelon blacks in white enterprises where this seemed desirable. The campaign for civil rights, and especially for Black Power, was not generally advanced by the trustees and presidents of Negro colleges. As a matter of fact, an increasing number of outbreaks in these colleges reflected the conflict, not between generations, but between forward- and backward-looking blacks.

An early example was the suspension of eight students at Alcorn Agricultural and Mechanical College at Lorman, Mississippi, in the spring of 1966, for engaging in civil rights activities. Charles Evers, a leader of the Mississippi NAACP, championed the victimized students and accused the Negro president of the college of being "only concerned with pleasing white folks." The students arose en masse and were supported by about 1,000 townsfolk, but state troopers used firehoses and tear gas to suppress the demonstration. Two years later, when Evers ran for Congress, Alcorn students passed out campaign literature and were dismissed from the school; 200 other students rallied in protest; again the troopers came in and quelled the disturbance with tear gas. Meanwhile, unrest had spread to dozens of other Negro colleges, including the most renowned—Howard and Tuskegee—and the first deaths on campus occurred at South Carolina State College at Orangeburg.

The outbreak of February 5, 1968, at Orangeburg, a town with two Negro colleges and the seat of a county with a two-thirds black population, was precipitated by the illegal segregation of a bowling alley. Students, probably under the influence of SNCC, demonstrated against the recreational center that refused to admit them. Governor Robert McNair called out the National Guard and state troopers, who clashed with the students. One student hit a trooper with a piece of lumber; other troopers opened fire on the students, killing three and injuring 35. The troopers said they thought that they were under sniper attack. The Governor said the students had taken guns from the ROTC armory, but the ROTC commanders said none were missing. Later it was agreed that the students had no guns.

Two days after the clash, Justice Department officials took steps to force the integration of the bowling alley. A month later black students and a few faculty members converged on South Carolina's state house and asked for redress, an increase in the appropriation for their college above the current $2.5 million, and a black majority on the Board of Trustees. They succeeded in obtaining only a letter from the Lieutenant Governor praising them for "following the normal, legal methods" in presenting their grievances, and a promise that the executive would ask for $6 million for the college.

The event revealed the stark fear among officials and the police of aroused black students. This fear was not diminished when the phantom student guns of Orangeburg became real guns a year later at Voorhees College in Denmark, South Carolina, 30 miles away. Governor McNair again called out the National Guard, this time to arrest a group of armed students who had already come to an agreement with the college president after having occupied part of the campus. When asked why they held guns, the students said, "We aren't going to allow another Orangeburg."

The trouble at Tuskegee began the last week of March, 1968, when the students presented a list of demands that included some rules changes and an end to compulsory ROTC. After temporary suspension of classes, the president made some concessions, but the trustees balked; and when they visited the campus on April 7, they were held captive in the guest house for about 12 hours until a threat to call the National Guard sobered the students. A few days later the end of ROTC training at Tuskegee and some other reforms were announced, and classes were resumed on April 22. The remarkable aspects of this event were the prestige of some of the captives—they included General Lucius Clay and Basil O'Connor—and the fact that the demands were unrelated to the contemporary struggle for Black Power.

The contrary was true at Howard, which had a history of minor disruptions. At the Charter Day ceremonies in 1967 the students had prevented General Lewis Hershey from making a speech. As a result, 16 students and five faculty members were dismissed, despite a student boycott of classes in protest against the penalty. President James M. Nabrit then announced that he would resign, but at the end of the year he retracted his offer. Early in 1968 he promised reforms in the area of student control over discipline, but he failed to carry out a pledge to announce the changes at the Charter Day ceremony on March 1. The students then took over the proceedings, and 39 of them were threatened with penalties for this act under the very rules that were to have been changed. The result was a mass sit-in at the administration building and occupation of the switchboard by 500 to 1,000 of the students for five days.

A full slate of demands was formulated, including Nabrit's resignation, "faculty control over academic affairs and student control over student affairs," and the organization of a curriculum with new emphasis on black studies. The president of the student council explained: "We want Howard University to begin to relate to the black community the way Harvard and MIT relate to the white community."

The trustees eventually agreed to meet some of the demands, particularly those involving student participation in disciplinary matters and amnesty for the demonstrators, and classes were resumed. The question of a relevant curriculum was one of many items discussed at a conference at Howard University, in mid-November, 1968, on the subject "Towards a Black University." Hundreds of black students from many colleges attended the five-day conference, with the largest attendance at the keynote address by Stokely Carmichael, who told them to "quit talking and start acting."

The first months of 1969 saw a flurry in the Howard medical and law schools (the latter including a brief sit-in and the resignation of Dean Patricia Roberts Harris, who complained that President Nabrit undercut her authority). A major revolt broke out early in May, when the campus was taken over for a day by the Black United Front, a joint student-community organization. The thrust and the mood had changed. The former student-power demands were supplemented by new demands for "community participation and involvement in the university" and courses that would make it possible for the students to become effective in the community. And the community–"nonstudents," in press terminology–participated in the action, which was ended by the arrival of police to enforce a court injunction.

The mutuality of interest between the black students at Howard and the surrounding black community was manifested by their joint struggle. It proved the validity of the students' demand for courses of study—black studies—that would enable them to function usefully, on their own terms, within their communities, and thus raise the level of the communities to approach that of comparable white communities. As the director of the black studies program at San Francisco State College pointed out, its purpose was to provide personnel who could "regenerate and reconstruct their own black communities, break the deadly grip of poverty and build a productive black future." The drive for integration, assimilation into a racist society, had been abandoned in favor of a drive to build within that society viable enclaves of Black Power. Some interpreted this as separatism, others visualized—in the spirit of Atlanta SNCC —a possible coalition between equals "at some later date."

The black intellectuals who made it to college had always been a privileged group among black people, and many of them recognized an obligation to serve their own community. That handful of black students who were admitted to white universities were likely to make an effort to "integrate"—a lonely and frustrating experience, usually— until enough of such students appeared on any campus to form a black group. When this occurred, morale improved, and eventually there developed not only a demand for black studies but also an attempt to expand the beachhead by bringing more brothers into the group and by reaching out toward a nearby black community. A black faculty member at the College of the City of New York commented on the mood among the insurgents on that campus in 1969:

They're very much concerned with the survival of the group, which is new. When I came along, the focus was on individual accomplishments. The feeling was that if you washed your face and learned to speak, the man would accept you. These kids now see that this is a lie if you're black or Puerto Rican. And they are now looking out for the group, not the individual. During the negotiations [with the administration], the man said, "All right, we'll give you enough money for your [black studies] program—you're safe," but they answered, "We are not safe if our brothers and sisters can't get in."

At Columbia University in April, 1968, both the SDS and the black students emphasized solidarity with the black community—in this case by opposing the building of a gymnasium in Morningside Park without adequate involvement of the Harlem residents who used the park. At about the same time the 20 or so black students at Trinity College in Hartford, Connecticut, held the president and six trustees captive in the administration building; the insurgents demanded scholarships for more blacks to enter the college (with an enrollment of about 1,600 whites) and courses in community development and the psychology of the ghetto. A similar demonstration with similar demands occurred that week at Boston University.

The following week about 100 blacks at Northwestern University in Evanston, Illinois, occupied a building until the administration acceded to most of their demands, which included recognition by the administration that "throughout its history it has been a university of white establishment." The blacks were granted their own living quarters for the following term and black counselors "to help us cope properly with the psychological, mental, and academic tensions" of a tiny minority in an unfriendly environment. This was probably the first request for black segregation, and its legality was dubious until a similar concession at Antioch in 1969 was cleared by the Federal government.

The confrontation at San Francisco State College—a respected unit of the state higher educational system accepting students unable to qualify for the University of California—had a number of unusual features, including a turnover of presidents. John Summerskill, who headed the college when disturbances first broke out in November, 1967, and refused to call police, was cashiered the next May and took a job in Ethiopia at the University of Addis Ababa. Robert Smith, his successor, was forced to resign in November, 1968, after closing the school to let it cool off following a series of disturbances largely provoked by the hostility of the trustees to a black English instructor. The trustees then appointed Samuel I. Hayakawa acting president; with the help of MACE- and gun-wielding city police, he opened the college on December 2, 1968.

Police occupied the campus until the end of April, 1969, during which time about 700 arrests were made. Governor Ronald Reagan gave enthusiastic support to Hayakawa's stern tactics, which were countered by a majority of the students, mostly blacks and members of other Third World minorities, principally Asian, Chicano, and American Indian, and by most of the teachers, who were on strike. Daily during the strike, 200 to 300 teachers phoned in sick, some 300 held classes as usual, and the remainder of the faculty taught in makeshift classrooms off campus. The principal demands were for a degree-granting department of black studies and open admission of black and Third World students. Nathan Hare, the black educator who had been hired to head the proposed black studies program, was one of those arrested. Hayakawa emerged as a hero of the hard-line set.

Cornell University was the scene of another series of confrontations, and its president, James Perkins, also became a national figure before abdicating, with an image almost the opposite of Hayakawa's. One of the first major universities to anticipate the trend without awaiting a major student revolt, Cornell had promised in September, 1968, to set up an Afro-American Studies Program. This plan was not implemented with sufficient speed, however, and in December the Afro-American Society staged a demonstration to needle the administration. Three of the participants were reprimanded by a student-faculty disciplinary committee whose jurisdiction they refused to recognize (not having participated in its selection), and the blacks showed their displeasure at the penalty by occupying Willard Straight Hall, the student center on campus.

During the night, after beating back an attack by a band of white fraternity students who sought to recapture the hall, the blacks sent for arms. When their terms were met by an administration representative the next morning, they evacuated the building. Photographs showing them as they left, bearing their guns, were featured in the nation's media and sparked a hysteria about blacks who seized university property "at gunpoint." The New York State legislators rushed to enact a law banning firearms on campus. (Only months earlier, in the wake of the assassination of Senator Robert F. Kennedy, the same legislature had refused to consider any kind of antigun legislation.)

Meanwhile, the agreement that brought about the surrender—a reversal of the reprimands—was itself reversed by the faculty, and the dean who had made the agreement resigned. A large meeting of students was held under SDS auspices and debated the situation all night. When it was clear that sentiment favored the blacks, the faculty met again and once more reversed itself, and the campus prepared to cool down. However, President Perkins was widely reviled as an appeaser, several faculty members resigned, and a few weeks later the blacks were arrested by local authorities on criminal charges. The principal outcome of the event was to feed the backlash and give rise to wild tales about campus guerrillas.

The spotlight turned at the end of April, 1969, on New York City, where Buell Gallagher of CCNY became a victim of his own ineptitude and pressure from politicos. In February, black and Puerto Rican students had briefly occupied the administration building to emphasize their demands: black and Puerto Rican studies; special "orientation" programs for black and Puerto Rican freshmen; student participation in the special (SEEK) program to prepare blacks and Puerto Ricans for entrance into the university; proportional admission of blacks and Puerto Ricans; and compulsory courses in black and Puerto Rican history for those at the university who were training to teach in the city, with its large proportion of black and Puerto Rican pupils. President Gallagher was reported to have said, "There was not a single one of these points which would not have been answered without yesterday's demonstration."

The students waited for two months, then lost patience and occupied the entire South Campus, closing the school.

Gallagher then set about negotiating with student leaders and their faculty sympathizers. Now the Board of Higher Education (holder of the purse strings), goaded by city politicians, lost patience in turn and ordered Gallagher to reopen the school. Rather than do so, he resigned; the police swarmed over the campus; and negotiations ended. The school was nominally open for business, but the presence of police, as usual, aroused many students who had not previously been concerned over the issues. White supporters developed a new tactic of "hit-and-run," disrupting classes just out of reach of the police, and once more the school closed.

The new president tried to adopt a hard line, overruling faculty recommendations to compromise, but finally felt obliged to proceed along the path opened by Gallagher. Negotiations were resumed, and a tentative agreement was reached granting the demands of the dissidents. The entire city was aroused, the faculty and students were split, all the political figures felt it necessary to issue statements attacking the agreement, and in the end it was whittled away to a compromise.

City College had admitted only applicants with extremely high scholastic averages. Since few ghetto schools turned out such graduates, the college had become a bastion of the elite white intelligentsia—and its alumni (who included leading politicians) wanted to keep it that way. But City College was also an inner-city unit of the City University and, according to another concept, it should serve the high school graduates of the less privileged areas without excessively emphasizing grades, even if this required a revamping of the institution's structure or an increase in its enrollment.

This was, in effect, what the blacks and Puerto Ricans demanded. Thus, the revolt at CCNY had forced a major confrontation between two concepts of the purpose of a public university—in itself no small service.

While the demand for increased black enrollment was under negotiation, a report was published by a joint commission sponsored by the Southern Education Reporting Service and the National Association of State Universities and Land Grant Colleges. It stated: "The conclusion that black Americans are grossly underrepresented in higher education seems inescapable," and presented incredible figures.

Four-fifths of all the state universities in the country are predominantly attended by whites. In these institutions, the percentage of blacks ranged from a low of 1.34 in the West (*not* the South) to a high of 2.98 in the Midwest. Probably less than 1 per cent of students receiving degrees in 1968 were black. In fact, there were more foreign students than black students in the entire United States higher education system.

Trend Toward Tandem

The participation of white students in the effort to bring more blacks into the colleges and to make the college curriculum more relevant to black students varied from campus to campus. The prevailing pattern was one of white support for black-initiated actions.

When 35 black students at Colgate University had a grievance against a discriminatory fraternity in April, 1968, 400 of the university's 1,800 white students and 35 of the faculty of 150 occupied the administration building; faculty

wives helped provide meals; and President Vincent Barnett
was moved to say: "This is a very unusual situation, a real
experience, in a sense a religious experience. . . . " He felt
that "the commitment of the white protestors to a Negro
cause and leadership seemed to have for many the emotional intensity of worship." A similar relationship between
blacks and a much smaller proportion of whites won the
victory at Northwestern in 1968. Whites were among the
1,300 students at the University of Texas who successfully
petitioned in November, 1967, for a course in Negro history. The first full-fledged black studies program at a major
Southern university was won at Duke in February, 1969,
when most of the campus blacks occupied an administration
building and were defended from police by some 1,000
white students outside the building; the whites later struck
classes for three days to protest against the police action.

Sometimes the whites took the initiative, as at Marquette
University, where they demonstrated in May, 1968, to urge
the university to take more interest in the black community
of Milwaukee; and at Iowa State in July, 1968, where
white students erected crosses in front of the administration building with the sign: "We are killing the spirit of
the black students."

But slowly the ways began to rift and part. At the
Columbia protest, the black students in Hamilton Hall asked
the whites to leave and conduct their own demonstration
for their own program—which happened to include the
"black" demand for abandonment of the gymnasium con-
struction. In later revolts, blacks and whites generally
conducted simultaneous but not coordinated actions. At
Harvard the black demand for an autonomous black studies

program, which was entirely successful, coincided with the routing of the white anti-ROTC protesters. At CCNY the SDS and other white radical support was subordinated to the black and Puerto Rican action, and no whites were represented among the negotiators.

Enemies of student activism made efforts to create or widen a gulf between the black and white camps, and had minor successes. The sally of the Greeks at Cornell against the black occupants of Willard Straight gladdened some who looked for a student antibody against the infection of revolt—but the stalwart white support of most Cornell students damped their glee. Brawls occurred at Queens College and City College in New York between embattled blacks and white counterinsurgents, but the white rebels were never enticed to rate skin over principles. The blacks and the whites in the movement tacitly agreed to work in tandem, to let each other do their own thing, and at times they welcomed, but did not necessarily seek, each other's support.

Actually, the programs had to be separate because, it was becoming clear, the goals were basically distinct. The blacks sought to use the white universities, as they hoped to use every white institution, to provide them with the tools they required for a dignified and effective role either in a black or (if they chose) in a white community. Black studies were not, as sometimes depicted, an ego-trip or a put-down of the whites. There was more to it than Swahili or ethnic art—there was an overdue rectification of history and a relevant social science. Nevertheless, within the black community, controversy arose as to whether the white universities should play host to such a curriculum. Building a suitable staff for black studies units (schools or departments) in the white colleges might soon drain the best black brains from the Negro institutions. In any case, this was a problem for the blacks to settle; they wanted no white advice.

The White Spectrum

The white camp also had its controversies. In the 1930's, student rebels had tended to affiliate with one or another of the contending radical factions—especially those of socialist or communist persuasion—and were, in effect, the campus sections of adult political organizations. This tendency faded before the menace of impending war, and the American Student Union of 1935 was radical but not political. In the 1960's, student rebels tended to band together on an ad hoc basis. Writes Robert A. Haber:

> In its early stages, student activity is neither very radical nor a very profound social protest. It generally does not go beyond a single issue, or see issues as inter-related, or stress that involvement in one issue necessarily leads to others. It does not, in short, seek root causes.

At first it seemed that the Free Speech Movement that developed at Berkeley in 1964 would become the model of the new type of student organization. Formed for a specific purpose, abandoned when its goal was apparently achieved, it suited the mood of the year. But as time passed, two of its component units, SNCC and SDS, became the centers around which a large number of the most concerned student activists rallied. Both were founded in 1960. SNCC became the spearhead of the first phase of civil rights activity on and off campus in the early 1960's, but with the passing of that phase (as previously recounted), its strength diminished.

Students for a Democratic Society was actually a new name for the student section of the venerable League for Industrial Democracy. But LID, with its "old left" spirit of anticommunist socialism, proved an unsuitable framework for the renascent student organization. Although the formal break did not come until 1966, by 1962 the SDS had already embarked on an independent course.

This course would be difficult to define. The SDS manifesto issued at its Port Huron convention in 1962 contributed the concept of "participatory democracy," which has remained an important ingredient in the student movement. This was especially a reaction against the impersonality of society and the university, which seemed to students pervasive, corrosive, antihuman, and intolerable. In its early years, and to some degree since, SDS sought to prove its concern by participating, not only in its immediate sector of society, the university, but in the civil rights movement and in neighboring communities. One of its ventures was the formation of the Economic Research and Action Project (ERAP), involving its members in organization of the poor in urban centers, such as Newark. At first the labor movement, through the United Auto Workers, helped them in this project. Later SDS began to try to forge a relationship with factory workers and to extend its organization to the high schools.

Before its 1969 convention in Chicago, SDS had no "philosophy" as an organization, and it made a point of welcoming a diversity of points of view. Its national organization made no attempt to impose discipline on local units (on more than 350 campuses in 1969), and each unit conducted its activities in a manner that seemed appropriate to the specific campus. The very looseness of the organization seemed to account for its spread; it became an umbrella under which any and every form of student protest could flourish. Therefore, whenever a group of students found cause to raise a banner, they tended to join or found a chapter of SDS. Its leaders spoke as individuals, retained as much authority as their immediate followers chose to assign, and displayed no lust for power.

Conventions of the SDS were debating sessions in which conflicting points of view were earnestly, heatedly, and inconclusively aired. It was an open-ended society of young people with tremendous turnover in membership and, despite its lack of ideology, far more impact on society than was ever achieved by its parent organization, the LID (which produced such respected leaders as Norman Thomas).

Most of the white-initiated demonstrations in the past few years were led, sponsored, guided, or supported by an SDS chapter on the campus involved. Yet that chapter, as the media have emphasized, in no sense represented the student body. It was always a tiny minority, usually far fewer than 100 out of thousands enrolled in the institution. What about the vast majority of the nation's 6,000,000-odd students?

They would seem to be a huge body of inert, unconcerned, and ineffective youth who neither approve nor condemn the impetus to change. Yet they inhabit the same world—the same society and the same campuses—as their more restless counterparts and are not entirely immune to the anxieties, the indignation, or the enthusiasms, that surge around them.

Sociologists would like to understand this problem. Those who have made an attempt to do so sometimes seem to cancel each other out. One authoritative specialist in the field of student activism, Professor Lewis Feuer, stresses the concept of generational conflict and suggests a revolt against authority, especially parental authority, that would tend to equate the rebellion of youth with hostility to the father. Another expert, however, Professor Seymour Martin Lipset (in a study written with Philip G. Altbach, formerly of the Comparative Student Project), points out:

> Studies of the backgrounds of activists indicate that the opposite, if anything, is true. They are much more often students who are acting out in practice the values which they have been taught by ideologically liberal parents. . . .

and Kenneth Keniston comes to a similar conclusion:

> When parents and their activist offspring disagree, it is usually not over principle but over practice; and when these students criticize their parents, it is not for what their parents believe, but for their failure to practice the beliefs they drummed into their children's ears from an early age. Thus "generational conflict" and rebellion against parents are gross oversimplifications applied to these students. . . .

When experts fall out, it is presumptuous for laymen to choose among them. The probability is that there is no simple explanation for the decision of this or that student to become active, to emerge from the conforming majority and enter the lists against the Establishment. There have been periods when such an impulse either failed to develop or was suppressed.

It is clear that certain individuals require more stimulation or different kinds of stimulation to respond to what

Keniston calls "a personal sense of ethical obligation to take a visible stand against injustice or oppression." The example of such a response by increasing numbers of one's fellows is contagious and—together with the growth and intensity of communications—probably accounts for the rapid development of the movement in the 1960's. Another factor, obvious from the occurrences on many campuses, has been a combination of administrative stupidity and faculty ambiguity, both manifestations of adult weakness that played into the hands of the rebels. A third factor was reaction to the use of force, which is always repugnant to youth, and to the frequently excessive degree of force, which enlisted large numbers of moderates in the activist camps—a process known as "radicalization" that was sometimes exploited by the radicals. The recipe for a successful rising would appear to comprise sufficient causes for discontent; a nucleus of activist students; a display of bad faith, bullying, or indifference (or a combination of these) on the part of the administration; and for a *pièce de resistance,* clubs and tear gas.

Thus, at Columbia in 1968, a large body of moderate students were converted to support the SDS, despite early disapproval of their occupation of campus buildings, once the authorities stumbled into a decision to bust the occupants:

> By its final days the revolt enjoyed both wide and deep support among the students and junior faculty and in lesser degree among the senior professors. The grievances of the rebels were felt equally by a still larger number, probably a majority, of the students. The trauma of the violence that followed police intervention intensified emo-

tions but support for the demonstrators rested upon broad discontent and widespread sympathy for the rebellion.

A Question of Power

The spread of student activism raised the specter of "student power"—the one issue that was rarely raised by the rebels themselves. As it turned out, a measure of student power was one of the clearest dividends resulting from the unrest.

The term properly refers to the participation of students in their campus community, on whatever level. In that sense, student government was an early, approved, and ineffective means of achieving the purpose. A major weakness of student government was the lack of interest in it usually shown by the students, who knew that the final power was firmly retained by the administration, sometimes in consultation with the faculty—if the faculty could be persuaded to show some interest in how the institution was run. Any student government that really set out to oppose either faculty or administration would be contemptuously ignored. The contempt was sometimes reciprocated: The Cornell students in 1968 elected a student government pledged to abolish student government!

In general, protesting students made no attempt (after the experience of SLATE at Berkeley) to "capture" the official organization. Instead, new ad hoc groups formed and, as occasional success came to SDS, that organization became the vehicle, the abrasive edge, for student-inspired changes on campus.

It was not consistent with either the SDS position or the temper of most restless students to seek the formation

of permanent relationships with the authorities, at least as
their immediate goal. (This failure, in official reporting, was
termed "lack of communications"—although little evidence
exists that the administration attempted to set up such
relationships except as a last resort.) Nor was there particular enthusiasm among students for long-range improvement
of the educational system—which, again, would seem the
responsibility of the faculty. However, the lists of student
demands sometimes included specific changes in the curriculum or manner of presenting courses, alterations in the
grading and examination procedures, and specific choices of
faculty members or even college presidents. There were other
signs of such interest. Concern about the university's role
in the war machine prompted Mario Savio to comment
in 1964, "It would be good to return to an almost totally
autonomous body of scholars and students." Another FSM
stalwart, Robert Starobin, said:

> Our idea is that the university is composed of faculty,
> students, books, and ideas. In a literal sense, the adminis-
> tration is merely there to make sure the sidewalks are kept
> clean. It should be the servant of the faculty and the
> students. We want a redemocratization of the university.
> Courses are clearly up to the faculty, but students should
> be able to convey their ideas.

Two years and hundreds of demonstrations later, the
Muscatine Report, issued by a faculty commission set up to
produce "specific proposals for the improvement of Berkeley education," was reviewed by Savio. He said that it
"failed to deal in any meaningful way" with important
criticisms that had been raised, and he concluded that the
report showed that

faculty members are consistently excluded from those groups of legislators, bureaucrats, and businessmen [the Regents] which make the most far-reaching decisions concerning the development and reform of the University. Those of us whose lives are directly involved are denied any effective voice in these decisions which structure and pervert our immediate environment. What has become of the "consent of the governed"? . . . It gives me little joy to say we were right. Perhaps students at other large universities can benefit from Berkeley's mistake. . . . No one can speak for students but students.

So students for the most part abandoned, as fruitless, efforts to reach the administration through official channels and achieved some reforms through less orthodox methods, about which more later. The first serious effort at a major institution to raise student-administration relations as an actual issue was made by a group that split from the striking student committee at Columbia in mid-May, 1968. Adopting the name of Students for a Restructured University, this group was soon awarded grants amounting to $30,000 to pursue their objective. Their effort culminated in the organization in 1969 of a University Senate of 101 members, of whom 21 were students. This body, with "the power to review the budget, pass on appointments of all high-level administrators and participate in the selection of some of the trustees," began to function on May 28, 1969, with a minimum of press coverage (page 29 of *The New York Times*). The first student contingent elected included representation from SRU but not from SDS.

The SDS defined its attitude toward the university in its Port Huron statement of 1962:

The university is located in a permanent position of social

influence. Its educational function makes it indispensable and automatically makes it a crucial institution in the formation of social attitudes. . . . it is the central institution for organizing, evaluating and transmitting knowledge. . . . a potential base and agency in the movement for social change.

As a relevant place for all the activities in which radicals should be engaged, according to SDS, the university is deserving of "reform by an alliance of students and faculty. They must wrest control of the educational process from the administrative bureaucracy . . . [and thus] build a base for their assault upon the loci of power."

While this language ("wrest control") is strong, there is still no hint of any scheme to destroy the institution. Such a position was first suggested by Mark Rudd, leader of the Columbia SDS in 1968. Rudd, who admitted that "We intend to make a revolution" and discounted the value of the university as either a base or a way-station toward this end, said:

> Student power is not the way to achieve a university structured to benefit humanity, since the problems of the university originate elsewhere. Because power and money are concentrated in corporations and government, it is impossible to create a "free" university within a society as unfree as ours; the university is the tool of society, or, in the American case, those who dominate our society. . . . To be sure, certain reforms are possible within the university, but these are mostly to give the illusion of democracy, as in student or faculty senate and judicial boards, or to grant more privileges to students, such as longer dormitory visiting hours or later curfew. University administrators can well afford to make such concessions, because of their lack of social significance.

This position was far beyond that of Port Huron. But insofar as it contemplated the destruction of the university, this was only incidental to the destruction of the entire Establishment. Rudd and his followers had no particular animus against the university as such.

But Rudd did not yet speak for SDS. His contemporary, past president Tom Hayden, said ". . . the university situation in America is more a symptom than a basic cause of our problems. But a college is one place to embark on a movement of reform, . . . a place from which reason might make a last attempt to intervene in human affairs." And Henry Norr, a leader of the Harvard SDS who sought a seat on the Board of Overseers: "It is not our purpose to destroy the university. We want universities that serve the whole population, not universities that function to legitimate the status quo."

Joel R. Kramer, president of the Harvard *Crimson,* a student paper, wrote a thoughtful article on the subject from the "moderate" point of view. His interpretation may be representative:

> "Student power" does not mean total control of the university. It does not mean the elimination of a university administration, or the elimination of faculty power. Students seek a shift in the balance of power. At most universities, the administration and trustees have most of the power, and the faculty has what is left. Students would like to see most of the power divided between themselves and the faculty.

A poll by the American Council on Education in 1968, using answers from 2,040 correspondents (its members and other educators), found general agreement that students will and should "serve as voting members on most important academic committees." And Fred M. Hechinger, educational editor of *The New York Times,* observed:

> The trend toward student participation in a wide variety of committees—from discipline to curriculum planning, and even in the selection of college presidents—is gaining momentum. Increasing numbers of institutions have established university-wide councils and senates, with student representatives.

The most strenuous student drive in this direction is found among the blacks, who insist that a black studies program cannot have validity unless it is "autonomous," i.e., directly controlled by the black students and faculty at the university. A major breakthrough was registered at Harvard, when its Faculty of Arts and Sciences voted in the spring of 1969 to allow black students to vote on the appointment of faculty for a projected black studies program. This was said to be "the first time that students have ever been given a direct role in the selection of faculty members at Harvard University."

The Question of Violence

Much emphasis is given to the tactics that have focused national attention on the weaknesses of the university. The media stressed whatever violence appeared. Yet no major movement for change has occurred in America with less violence, in relation to the amount of reform accomplished and the gravity of the ills still to be remedied, than the student movement of the 1960's.

Students have been imaginative, but they have not invented any tactic in their effort to achieve their purposes.

Their entire arsenal was borrowed from unionists and free-dom fighters: petition, picketing, demonstration, stike, and sit-in. The effort attributed to the FSM to bring the uni-versity "to a grinding halt" can be compared to that of any union to stop production in a factory—which, to be sure, was damned in its day as intolerable. The inconvenience to students who wish to go to class as usual, unmolested, can be compared to the annoyance of consumers who are de-prived of services or goods withheld as the result of a stike. A black student blockading the CCNY campus told an impatient white student: "So you lost a day, a week, or a semester. We've lost generations and, damn it, this is what we intend to stop."

Actually, the only serious violence in the campus "dis-orders" has been brought about by the forces of law and order—whether at Orangeburg, resulting in the first fatalities; at Columbia and Harvard, where the police overreaction served to radicalize the moderates; or at Berkeley in 1969, where a National Guard helicopter confused Sproul Plaza with a jungle of Southeast Asia.

The fervid controversy concerning "violence" is no sub-stitute for a serious analysis of just how and why certain tactics were evolved. Several observers have pointed out that the lessons of the labor and civil rights movement were consciously adopted, and this is confirmed by statements of the participants—Jack Weinberg at Berkeley, for example:

There have been wildcat strikes which in many ways are quite similar to the Free Speech protest. . . . The union has proven itself incapable of dealing with the issue. Then one day a work practice is changed or a worker is penal-ized over a minor infraction. Fellow workers protest and are either ignored or reprimanded. A wildcat strike is called and the protest is on. The same kind of force which creates a wildcat strike has created the FSM. Alienation and hostility exist, but are neither focused at specific grievances nor well articulated. . . . Suddenly there is an issue; everyone recognizes it; everyone grabs at it. A feeling of solidarity develops among the students. . . .

The debt to the civil rights experiences was stated explicitly by Mario Savio:

> Last summer I went to Mississippi to join the struggle there for civil rights. This fall I am engaged in another phase of the same struggle, this time in Berkeley. . . . The same rights are at stake in both places—the right to participate as citizens of a democratic society and the right to due process of law. . . . We have encountered the organized status quo in Mississippi, but it is the same at Berkeley. Here we find it impossible usually to meet with anyone but secretaries. Beyond that, we find functionaries who cannot make policy but can only hide behind the rules. We have discovered total lack of response on the part of the policy makers.

This sense of frustration, of failing to "communicate" with the "bureaucracy," of the futility of seeking redress through the "chain of command" (reminiscent of the Declaration of Independence: " . . . such has been the patient sufferance of these Colonies . . . "), pervades many accounts of the first, nonviolent, phase of campus revolt. Witness the Cox report on Columbia:

> . . . the faculty became more and more remote from problems of student life. . . . The authoritarian manner on one side, and aloofness, on the other, were mutually reinforcing. . . . The faculty as a body and most of its members

as individuals failed to speak out upon matters of intense student concern. . . . the faculty's lack of concern for the non-curricular interests and needs of students were all too evident to students themselves. . . . the scale of priorities at Columbia all too regularly put the students' problems at the bottom. . . . We are persuaded that the faculty's remoteness and its lack of vigilance *vis-à-vis* the Administration were significant factors in the development of an atmosphere in which student unrest could reach the point of combustion.

The report, although aware of the faculty's "lack of vigilance *vis-à-vis* the Administration," limited its criticism of the administration to scattered and generalized observations. There is reference to "the constant improvisation to which the Administration was driven in dealing with student problems. . . ." There are instances of deliberate display of contempt of the student on the part of the administration, best illustrated by the widely quoted statement of the vice-dean of Graduate Facilities ("widely regarded as a spokesman of the Administration"): ". . . whether students vote 'yes' or 'no' on an issue is like telling me they like strawberries." There is an estimate of the manner in which President Kirk handled the Committee on Student Life report: ". . . the way the report was treated conveyed an authoritarian style and unmistakable message. The resentment and frustrations they generated not only sparked the radicals but go far to explain why so many more moderate students joined in or supported even April's extreme demonstration." But there is no thoughtful delineation of the chain of circumstances that almost duplicated those at Berkeley four years earlier (a record evidently not consulted by scholars). the arbitrary dictum of the Kirk Directives, arbitrarily applied against

selected victims; the duplicity in the matter of IDA; the
persistent reluctance to deal reasonably with students, however dissident. The Cox Report had to come to a reluctant
conclusion:

> One final point concerning the three avowed issues should
> be noted. On none of them had SDS made a genuine effort
> to exhaust the peaceful forms for shaping a great uni-
> versity's course of action. We are not unmindful that the
> formal structure of Columbia's institutions, the apparent
> detachment of the faculty, and the record of the Trustees
> and Administration made these alternatives such discouraging
> prospects that no one should be very surprised that they
> were ignored.

The inaccessibility for which President Kirk was noted
was, of course, only one factor in the complex prelude to
the Columbia uprising. But it was not peculiar to Kirk—
it was, and is, an occupational malady. An anecdote related
by a student at Lewis and Clark College in Oregon illustrates what students had to face almost everywhere:

> They were building a new chapel at our school, which quite
> a few students didn't think was necessary; it was a waste
> of money. So during the dedication ceremony, about two
> hundred people demonstrated against it—very quietly, very
> respectfully—they just held up their signs. But the president
> got up and said, "OK, now we've seen their point, they
> don't like it." Then they went right ahead—no more discus-
> sion ever again—and the chapel is now half finished. He
> spoke one sentence about it in his entire speech. He ac-
> knowledged there was a demonstration. And that was the
> end.

The next phase appears in another story, told by Arthur
Schlesinger, Jr. A meeting of the Board of Trustees at
Antioch College was attended by some 75 students, who

interrupted the official proceedings with an outrageous display of horseplay. Eventually most of the students filed out, and the session was allowed to continue:

> A moment of silence followed. Then the trustee who had been reading the report from the committee on investigations resumed exactly where he had left off. This was too much for a colleague, who broke in and said reasonably, "Mr. Chairman, I don't think we ought to act as if nothing had happened." The chairman asked what he proposed, and the trustee suggested that they invite the students who had remained to tell them what this demonstration had been all about. The students still in the room responded that, while they had not approved of the demonstration, they were delighted that it had forced the trustees to listen to them. "You may not like what you saw," one student remarked. "But now you are discussing things that you would never be discussing on your own initiative." And for the first time the Antioch board of trustees permitted on its agenda some of the problems that were worrying Antioch students.

At the risk of overstressing the obvious, it may be worthwhile to add Schlesinger's observations:

> This story illustrates a disastrous paradox: The extremist approach works. "I feel like I just wasted three and a half years trying to change this university," a Columbia senior said after the troubles of last spring [1968]. "I played the game of rational discourse and persuasion. Now there's a mood of reconstruction. All the log-jams are broken— violence pays. . . ." The activists understand what has until recently escaped the attention of the deans—that a small number of undergraduates, if they don't give a damn, can shut down great and ancient universities. As a result, when the activists turn on, the administrators at last begin to do things which, if they had any sense, they would have done on their own long ago. . . .

One may question whether the activists "don't give a damn." This charge is less likely to be thrust at the spokesmen for the approved student governments who become NSA officers. Yet such students, attending by invitation a conference in Pittsburgh of the Academy of Religion and Mental Health to give testimony on the campus crisis, "noted that the sessions in which they participated had the poorest attendance. They complained that the professionals were all in other meeting rooms talking to one another instead of listening to them." The vice-president of the NSA said: "This is one of the root causes of the youth rebellion, the attitude that the older generation takes toward us. You people are supposed to be professional communicators, but you do not want to listen to us."

That same day the president of the University of Minnesota, Malcolm C. Moos, told a meeting of newspapermen:

> Universities have been slow and unresponsive in many areas in developing reforms—quick to study others, slow to study themselves. We fuel the destructive notion that disruption is the path to reform by moving under threat of chaos and doing business as usual when tensions seem low.

To expand the horizon of interpretation of the causes of violence on campus, let us consider a summary in the *Saturday Review* by editor Norman Cousins:

> . . . any careful study of the rapidity with which student demonstrations and protest have degenerated into violence will have to consider the extent to which the society itself has become a school for violence. . . . A President of the United States and a great civil rights leader are killed with guns that can be bought through the mail or over the counter, yet it is impossible to get enough support to

prohibit the sale of such weapons. . . . Villages in Vietnam have been systematically destroyed and countless thousands of people have become homeless; the reasoning is
that this will save them from marauding Vietcong. . . . Is
it possible, in short, to detach completely the disruptive
actions of young people from the violence that surrounds
them and that indeed is fed to them with the blessings of
their elders? . . . One suspects that the basic causes of vio-
lent protest are to be found in the mirror.

It is well to preserve a distinction between "disruptive
actions," which campus youth certainly have employed, and
"violence," which has been rare and of low intensity. The
events at Berkeley, for example, aroused storms of revulsion,
a number of faculty resignations, an extensive controversy
in the media (including magazine articles and books), and
hardly any improvement in the situation on that campus.
But the students who surged around the police car took
care to remove their shoes before climbing atop the vehicle
to speak to the crowd!

This spirit of politeness wilted before the affront of clubs
and tear gas, and later confrontations undeniably included
moments of barbarism on the student side. The manhandling
of a dean at Harvard and a mild indignity to President
Perkins of Cornell were conspicuous because of their depar-
ture from the usual respect to the person shown by student
activists. Attacks on books and card files, wanton arson,
graffiti, are revolting evidences of frustration, but the causes
of the frustration were usually more revolting and less justified or likely to be remedied. Perkins showed rare understanding of the blacks with guns who emerged from Willard
Straight Hall when he explained that they feared an ambush.
The history of the treatment of blacks in similar circum-

stances does not make this fear as unreasonable, for example, as the panic of the Cornell professors who fled to motels lest the spirit of Nat Turner reincarnate on their campus.

One must consider the point that most campuses have escaped all overt manifestations of unrest. A survey of three serene campuses appeared in the spring of 1969. Suffolk College, in Boston, where 4,000 day and night students are enrolled, does not literally have a campus; it lacks both student center and gymnasium. The editor of the student magazine says: "We're middle or lower middle class here. People come here to get a diploma which is a passport to a job with Sylvania or IBM. In Suffolk, that passport is the most important thing in the world."

The rural counterpart is represented by the University of North Dakota at Grand Forks, with 7,500 enrolled. The student editor reports: "The campus is still the American dream. People come here to get a normal education and graduate and leave the state for the west or Minneapolis and find a job with IBM or Control Data and get ahead and live comfortably and serenely." A fraternity student speaks: "You see, most of us are not here to change the world but to get a degree and maybe in the process learn something." When a black militant appeared on campus, one student reacted thus: "I walked away almost sick . . . when I heard him because I've realized that he made a good case, that maybe I'm a racist and I don't want to be one and I don't know what to do about it." A sorority girl comments: "There's nothing really to demonstrate about at this school and on certain issues, like Vietnam, well, I haven't really taken sides."

The least typical of the three, perhaps, is the Franklin and Marshall campus at Lancaster, Pennsylvania, with 1,700 enrolled. Its president, Keith Spalding, "meets with students in his home, has hired a black recruiter to seek out ghetto youths, has placed students on virtually every administration committee and is discussing with the school's 60 black students the creation of a black studies and cultural center." According to an SDS leader on campus, "The administration has this great pacification program—they sound nice and liberal, they placate everybody. . . ."

A famous participant in the debate on student disruption was the Rev. Theodore Hesburgh, president of Notre Dame, whose hard-line ultimatum was applauded by President Richard Nixon, among others. Notre Dame seems to have followed the Franklin and Marshall model. There were protests in 1960 against an 11 o'clock curfew, which was abandoned when "19 fellowship nominees threatened to publish a critical 80-page report on the university." The administration cracked down on a student government report in 1963, but five years later acceded to the within-the-university changes urged in that report. A demonstration by the organized blacks on campus was sidetracked by capitulation and the establishment of a black studies program. According to one graduate, "Political power at Notre Dame does not grow from the barrel of a gun but from the drum of a mimeograph machine." No one accused Hesburgh of buckling under or compared him with Cornell's Perkins. Nor was the publicity accorded to the earlier "tough" statement by Father Hesburgh given to the following remarks by Notre Dame's astute president:

God bless these difficult, demanding revolutionary students, who are the reason and often the despair of our educational existence. We find it difficult to live with them but without them there would be little reason for institutions. Their desire for involvement is good, as it affects their education, their student government, their extracurricular life, their concern that the university be a community in which they have a real and not a fictitious part. I believe that we can establish structures that give them involvement and voice in all of these matters without instantly conferring on them the earned competence that is the prerogative of trustees. We should involve students in every legitimate way to the extent that they are willing to assume responsibility, as well as to assert their rights. The results should ultimately be measured by their growth in maturity, insight and creativity and the basic standard should be educational development. We must take some chances and have more faith in this younger generation and have more understanding of their concerns.

CHAPTER SEVEN

ASSESSMENT

THIS IS A PERIOD in which the nation is reappraising its position on a number of key questions. Among these are the role of the United States in the world; the pace of realization of civil rights, in practice as well as in theory; and the possibility of applying abundant resources to the final elimination of poverty. These questions are, without doubt, on the agenda. To what extent have the universities responded to them?

There is a myth that universities are the sites of dispassionate evaluation among scholars concerning the vital issues before society. This myth has been evoked by the harshest critics of student activism, one of whom, George F. Kennan, is distressed by young people "screaming, throwing stones, breaking windows, overturning cars, being beaten or dragged about by police" when they should, instead, "give years of disciplined and restrained study, years of the scholars' detachment, years of readiness to reserve judgment while evidence is being accumulated." Kennan is appalled at the damage threatened to his ideal of a university by these "*enragés*." And what is this ideal?

231

> It is the ideal of the association of the process of learning
> with a certain remoteness from the contemporary scene—a
> certain detachment and seclusion, a certain voluntary with-
> drawal and renunciation of participation in contemporary
> life in the interests of the achievement of a better perspec-
> tive on that life when the period of withdrawal is over.

This seems an odd prescription for a center of higher education toward the end of the 20th century. It might have been
appropriate to an era when the function of higher education
was to train an elite to manage a secure Establishment. It
requires no perspective to conclude that this era has long
since passed in the United States.

In any case, the embattled students are not attempting to
destroy this ideal university, because it no longer exists and
has not existed for more than a century. It was destroyed,
utterly and irreversibly, in the process of development of
which most scholars are more aware than most students,
and which we have attempted to trace in this book.

The university has faced crises before, and sometimes sur-
mounted them. The medieval university, however, was seduced by the Establishment—and the intellectual work of the
world was done elsewhere:

> Much of the Renaissance occurred completely outside the
> university. The university was generally enlisted against
> the Reformation, although bitter fights were fought within
> many universities and in some the reformers emerged tri-
> umphant. The industrial, democratic, and scientific revolu-
> tions have gradually moved in on the universities and
> changed them almost beyond recognition. . . . In all these
> intellectual and social revolutions, the university, as an
> institution, was initially more "a stronghold of reaction"
> than a revolutionary force, although the ideas of its indi-
> vidual members have often been a stimulus to change.

It is instructive that this observation was made by Clark Kerr, as the student revolts were imminent. Kerr distinctly symbolized the virtues and defects of the keen scholar, who can at the same time grasp and fail to cope with crises. As the students were about to force his university to adapt itself to changes in society, Kerr cited Frederick Rudolph thus:

> Resistance to fundamental reform was ingrained in the American collegiate and university tradition, as over three hundred years of history demonstrated. . . . Except on rare occasions, the historic policy of the American college and university [was]: drift, reluctant accommodation, belated recognition that while no one was looking, change had in fact taken place.

Of course, change did occur throughout the later history of the college and university, as we have had occasion to notice. Not all of this change was for the better, but the enlargement of the curriculum and of registration rolls and even the concepts, if not the practice, of the research and service functions must be included on the credit side. A faculty loyal to its traditional role might have helped direct intellectual resources toward fruitful objectives while continuing to teach. But the society in which they operated offered stronger incentives to abstain from this obligation. That same society, however, provided another component of the university world whose interests were directly related to changing their environment constructively: the students.

The students who took up the challenge—and these, it is understood, were a minority of their generation—were thoroughly motivated. The white students, many of them from affluent homes and certain of material acceptance after graduation (providing they escaped death in Vietnam), were under no pressure of the sort that intimidated earlier generations. They could afford the perspective needed to judge contemporary society, including their university environment and the values of the preceding generation (their parents). Some of them outraged that generation by decrying those values. Others adopted a principled stand, not unusual among youth (who are expected to be briefly "idealistic"), against the most obvious hypocrisies, or indulged their need to experiment in the adult world by playing a part in real-life events such as Freedom Rides instead of on the athletic fields. The black students were riding the crest of a wave of frustrated hopes—they were part of a broad movement in a most dynamic stage. All American youth shared with the rest of the world's youth, who were in simultaneous rebellion on a variety of issues, a sense that there was little time, in the world's history, for many more mistakes.

The academic community recoiled from the attack, not recognizing in it the assumption of an obligation on which they had defaulted. However, a dim recognition penetrated part of the faculties, usually those with least commitment (in tenure, grants, published posture) toward the Establishment. The account of some of the events illustrates this ambiguity. One never knew whether the teachers would approve or censure, and one never knew whether the administration would be influenced by a faculty vote—teachers' preferences concerning strawberries might also be irrelevant. Occasionally an educator of some eminence would show a glimmer of comprehension. One such was the maverick former president of Sarah Lawrence, Harold Taylor:

> If the university and its present leadership fail to act, either to stop the war, to reform the archaic curriculum, to grant legitimate student rights, to take its students seriously, to

take a stand against racism and racial injustice, then what else can serious people do, students or anyone else, than to move beyond acquiescence into protest and resistance? The power of the social and intellectual force within the new generation of students has been greatly under-estimated by educators and the public, who have tended to think of student activists and those concerned with civil rights and world affairs as a general nuisance. . . . On the contrary, what we have is a new and significant national asset. In fact, the core of the student protest movement is composed of a serious and informed body of young people . . . responsible critics of this society and its educational system, and the best of them have a political sophistication and social energy which is in advance of many of those appointed to educate them.

Taylor was particularly discerning when he pointed out that student criticism was simultaneously directed against the educational system *and* society. Inasmuch as the outbreaks occurred mainly on campus, an assumption developed that the universities were the main if not the only target, and the achievement of the student activists was measured in terms of changes in the universities. These were considerable—far beyond anything envisaged by either the faculties or the administrations, who would have preferred to devote decades to "achievement of a better perspective." Tangible reforms included programmatic and curricular changes (especially in the social sciences and as related to the blacks), procedural changes in measuring achievement, structural changes involving student participation at various levels, but most of all an awareness that students meant to restore some of their ancient and almost forgotten privileges. No university could function without taking them into consideration—and this undoubtedly brought delight to many on the faculty who would not have lifted a hand to bring it about, for it indirectly favored the professors *vis-à-vis* the administration in that long-waged contest for power.

But the university has become a linchpin within the social structure and must be made secure against what the Establishment considers subversion. The howls of outrage emanating from businessmen, professional men, political figures, reaching into the legislatures and executive mansions, are not caused by any devotion toward higher education as a citadel of learning—its motivation is fear *lest* the university once more assume that role and make it necessary to construct a parallel system of laboratories, institutions, experimental stations and similar paraphernalia frankly devoted to the service of the military-industrial complex. It would be so difficult to organize, pay for, and staff such a system, outside of the universities, that the prospect is unthinkable. It is in this area—the disestablishment of ROTC, of the war-related research and development programs, of on-campus employment agencies for the Pentagon and aerospace and CBW industries—that the occasional successes of the students struck a nerve and provoked a backlash.

This backlash has taken the form of intimidation, the threat of reprisal against institutions and individuals who fail to suppress manifestations of student unrest. The students themselves are not likely to succumb, especially since the activist mood has spread into the high schools, and the oncoming generation may be even more revolt-prone than the current one. The question is whether the faculties will seize the opportunity to restore the integrity of the universities, by re-examining the functions of these institutions in relation to the students, to the world of the intellect, and to society.

REFERENCE NOTES

TEXT REFERENCES are identified below by page number and order of appearance.

3   Dana Carleton Munro and Raymond James Sontag, *The Middle Ages* (Century, 1921), p. 367

5   Helene Wieruszowski, *The Medieval University* (Van Nostrand, 1966), p. 136 (all medieval documents cited are translations by Wieruszowski.)

6   *Ibid.,* pp. 123–124

8   *Ibid.,* p. 134

8–9   *Ibid.,* p. 32

11–12   *Ibid.,* pp. 198–199

14   *Ibid.,* pp. 170–171 and p. 167

15   *Ibid.,* p. 179

15–16   *Ibid.,* p. 157

18   *Ibid.,* p. 142

18–19   *Ibid.,* pp. 192–193

19   John P. Davis, *Corporations* (Capricorn, 1961), Vol. I p. 303 n. 1

21–22   *Ibid.,* Vol. II p. 4

22–23   Wieruszowski, *op. cit.,* p. 133

23   *Ibid.,* p. 191

28   William Boyd, *The History of Western Education* (Barnes and Noble, 8th ed. 1966), p. 281

32   Frederick Rudolph, *The American College and University* (Vintage, 1965), p. 8

33   J. B. Mullinger, *A History of the University of Cambridge,* cited by Richard Hofstadter, *Academic Freedom in the Age of the College* (Columbia University Press, 1955), p. 74 n. 177

34   Author of *New England First Fruits* (1643), cited by Rudolph, *op. cit.,* pp. 3–4

34   Carl A. Lohmann, "Yale University," in *Encyclopedia Americana* (1961)

34   Edmund S. DeLong, "Princeton University," in *Encyclopedia Americana* (1961)

36   Samuel Sewall, *Diary,* cited by Hofstadter, *op. cit.,* p. 101 n. 40

38   Rudolph, *op. cit.,* p. 32

40–41   Samuel Eliot Morison, *Three Centuries of Harvard* (Harvard University Press, 1946), pp. 70–71

42   *Ibid.,* pp. 102–103, p. 104, and p. 41

43   *Ibid.,* pp. 117–118 and p. 133

44   *Ibid.,* p. 146

48   Rudolph, *op. cit.,* p. 44

49   *Ibid.,* p. 48 and p. 56

52   Walter C. Bronson, *History of Brown University,* cited by Rudolph, *op. cit.,* p. 181

53–54   The Yale Report as published in *The American Journal of Sciences and Arts* (XV, 1829), cited by Rudolph, *op. cit.,* pp. 132–134 (four citations)

54   Pamphlet of 1825, cited by Rudolph, *op. cit.,* p. 122

55   Dirk J. Struik, *The Origins of American Science (New England)* (Cameron Associates, 1948), p. 149

56   *Ibid.,* p. 245

56   Edwin S. Burdell, "Cooper Union," in *Encyclopedia Americana* (1961)

56   Palmer C. Ricketts, *History of Rensselaer Polytechnic Institute 1824–1914,* cited by Rudolph, *op. cit.,* p. 230

58   Struik, *op. cit.,* p. 160

58   Rudolph, *op. cit.,* p. 272

58   Cited by Morison, *op. cit.,* p. 287

59   Cited by Struik, *op. cit.,* p. 348

60   Walter P. Metzger, *Academic Freedom in the Age of the University* (Columbia University Press, 1955), p. 30

62   James Harris Fairchild, cited in *Documentary History of American Higher Education* (1961) by Richard Hofstadter and Wilson Smith, Vol. I pp. 428–429

63   Marshall B. Davidson, *Life in America* (Houghton Mifflin, 1951), Vol. II p. 360 (citing John Elliot writing to Jeremy Bellknap)

64   Hofstadter, *Academic Freedom* . . . , p. 124

65   John S. Brubacher and Willis Rudy, *Higher Education in Transition* (Harper, 1958), p. 51

65   Andrew Dickson White, *Autobiography*, cited by Brubacher and Rudy, *op. cit.*, p. 54

65   Morison, *op. cit.*, pp. 230–231

66   *Ibid.*, pp. 260–261

66   Brubacher and Rudy, *op. cit.*, p. 103

66   Walter C. Bronson, *op. cit.*, cited by Rudolph, *op. cit.*, p. 172

67   Morison, *op. cit.*, p. 162

67–68   *Ibid.*, p. 253

69   Frederick Rudolph, *Mark Hopkins and the Log: Williams College, 1836–1872* (Yale University Press, 1956), p. *vii*

76   Cited by Frank C. Abbott, *Government Policy and Higher Education* (Cornell University Press, 1958), p. 46

77   Cited by Rudolph, *The American College* . . . , p. 256

78   Cited *ibid.*, p. 255

78   Morison, *op. cit.*, p. 328

78–79   *Ibid.*, p. 304

85   Rudolph, *op. cit.*, p. 331

86   Cited by Rudolph, *op. cit.*, p. 333

87   J. T. Metz, *European Thought in the Nineteenth Century*, cited by Boyd, *op. cit.*, p. 336

87   Cited by Rudolph, *op. cit.*, p. 352

90   Charles A. and Mary Beard, *The Rise of American Civilization* (Macmillan, 1930), Vol. II, p. 478

94   Noah Porter, *The American Colleges and the American Public*, cited by Rudolph, *op. cit.*, p. 429

95   Beard, *op. cit.*, Vol. II, p. 470

96   Brubacher and Rudy, *op. cit.*, p. 322

97   Rudolph, *op. cit.*, pp. 438–439

98   *Ibid.*, p. 196

99   *Ibid.*, p. 400

100   Metzger, *op. cit.*, p. 112

101   Dixon Ryan Fox, *Union College, An Unfinished History*, cited by Brubacher and Rudy, *op. cit.*, p. 45

102   "What Is a College For?" in *Scribner's* (1909), cited by Brubacher and Rudy, *op. cit.*, p. 116

103   Brubacher and Rudy, *op. cit.*, p. 45

105   Rudolph, *op. cit.*, p. 151

106   *Ibid.*, p. 153

106   Kent Sagendorph, *Michigan: The Story of a University*, cited by Rudolph, *op. cit.*, pp. 373–374

107   Everett Lee Hunt, *The Revolt of the College Intellectual* (Human Relations Aids, 1963), p. 44

108   Cited by Hunt, *op. cit.*, pp. 48 f.

109   Cited by Frances E. Falvey, *Student Participation in College Administration* (Columbia University Press, Teachers College, 1952), pp. 46–47

110   Gordon John Klopf, *College Student Government* (Harper, 1960), p. 41

114–115 Daniel Bell, *The Reforming of General Education* (Columbia University Press, 1966), p. 96

115   Christopher Jencks and David Riesman, *The Academic Revolution* (Doubleday, 1968), p. 61 and p. 130

118   Bell, *op. cit.*, pp. 74–76

120   Clark Kerr, "The Frantic Race to Remain Contemporary," in *The Contemporary*

University, ed. by Robert S. Morison (Beacon, 1964), p. 27

122   Robert S. Morison, "Foundations and Universities," *The Contemporary University*, p. 94

122   Kerr, *op. cit.*, p. 27

122–123 Hugh S. Brown and Lewis B. Mayhew, *American Higher Education* (Center for Applied Research in Education, Inc., New York, 1965), p. 71

124   James Ridgeway, "Universities as Big Business," in *Harper's* (September, 1968)

125   John Fischer's "Easy Chair" in *Harper's* (August, 1968)

125   Kerr, *op. cit.*, pp. 31–32

127   Robert S. Morison, preface to *The Contemporary University*, p. x

127   Bell, *op. cit.*, p. 19

127   Jencks and Riesman, *op. cit.*, p. 512

129   Bell, *op. cit.*, p. 19

129   Brubacher and Rudy, *op. cit.*, p. 261

130   Rudolph, *op. cit.*, p. 460

131–132 Cited by Samuel Eliot Morison, *op. cit.*, p. 444

133   Report on College Plans of the Carman Committee cited by Bell, *op. cit.*, p. 23

136   Esther Raushenbush, "A Larger Role for the Small College," in *Harper's* (August, 1968)

138   Jencks and Riesman, *op. cit.*, p. 63 and p. 104

141–142 Harold Taylor, address at World Affairs Conference, University of Colorado at Boulder, cited in *The New York Times* (May 5, 1968) and also in *The Berkeley Student Revolt*, p. 62

142   Fischer, *op. cit.*

145   Jencks and Riesman, *op. cit.*, p. 43 and p. 37

146   Hofstadter, *op. cit.*, p. 204

147   Rudolph, *op. cit.*, p. 287

147   Lewis S. Feuer, *The Conflict of Generations* (Basic Books, 1969), p. 324

148   Kenneth Keniston, "The Faces in the Lecture Room," in *The Contemporary University*, p. 325

149   *Look* magazine (April 2, 1968)

150   Mary N. Gonzales, "A Vote for Student Protest," in *Notes From the Troubled Campus* introduced by Edward A. Weeks for the editors of *Atlantic Monthly* (1965)

150   John Reed, "Almost Thirty," in the *New Republic* (April 29, 1936), cited by Feuer, *op. cit.*, p. 350

151   Cited by Jeremy Larner, "Nobody Knows . . . Reflections on the McCarthy Campaign," in *Harper's* (April, 1969)

151   Feuer, *op. cit.*, p. 343, p. 342, and p. 347 (three citations)

152   SLID pamphlet, "Students in Revolt" (1933)

152–153 James Arthur Wechsler, *Revolt on the Campus*, (Kovici-Friede, 1935), pp. 15–16

153   Alan Valentine, *Trial Balance* (Pantheon, 1956), cited by Hunt, *op. cit.*, p. 50

155–156 Wechsler, *op. cit.*, pp. 95–96

156–157 James K. Feibleman, "What Happens in College," in *Saturday Review* (October 20, 1962), reprinted in *The American Student and His College*, ed. by Esther Lloyd-Jones and Herman E. Estrin (Houghton-Mifflin, 1967)

157   Cited by Wechsler, *op. cit.*, p. 49

159   *Ibid.*, p. 144 and pp. 387–388

160–161 *Ibid.*, pp. 348–350

163   Falvey, *op. cit.*, p. 9 and pp. 12–13

163   Klopf, *op. cit.*, p. 41

163   Jencks and Riesman, *op. cit.*, p. 57

164   Sol Stern, "NSA and the CIA," in *Ramparts* magazine (March, 1967)

165   Michael Wood in *Ramparts* (March, 1967)

166   Cited in *Chronicles of Black Protest*, ed. by Bradford Chambers (New American Library, 1969), p. 179

166   Howard Zinn, *SNCC: The New Abolitionists* (Beacon Press, 1965), p. 16

167   Ibid., p. 26

168   Paul Jacobs and Saul Lindau, *The New Radicals* (Vintage, 1966), pp. 12–13
168   Henry May, "The Student Movement at Berkeley: Some Impressions," in *The Berkeley Student Revolt,* ed. by Seymour Martin Lipset and Sheldon S. Wolin (Anchor, 1965), p. 459
168–169   A. H. Raskin, "The Berkeley Affair: Mr. Kerr vs. Mr. Savio & Co.," in *The New York Times Magazine* (Feb. 14, 1965), reprinted in *The Berkeley Student Revolt,* p. 429
169   David Riesman, "Where Is the College Generation Headed?", reprinted in *The American Student and His College*
169–170   Dale L. Johnson, "On the Ideology of the Campus Revolution," in *Studies on the Left* (Vol. II No. 1, 1961), reprinted in Jacobs and Landau, *op, cit.,* pp. 99–100
170   Clark Kerr, *The Uses of the University* (Harvard University Press, 1963), reprinted in *The Berkeley Student Revolt,* p. 47 and p. 56
171   FSM pamphlet, "We Want a University," reprinted in Hal Draper, *Berkeley: The New Student Revolt* (Grove, 1965)
171–172   Jack Weinberg, "The Free Speech Movement and Civil Rights," in *Campus CORE-lator* (January, 1965), reprinted in Draper, *op. cit.,* pp. 187–188
173   Ken Cloke and Roger Hollander, cited by Max Reirich and Sam Kaplan, "Yesterday's Discord," in *California Monthly* (February, 1965), reprinted in *The Berkeley Student Revolt,* p. 26
173   Reirich and Kaplan, *op. cit.,* p. 22
174   *Ibid.,* p. 33
175   Chancellor Edward W. Strong, cited in "Chronology of Events: Three Months of Crisis," by the editors of *California Monthly,* in *The Berkeley Student Revolt,* p. 114
176   Report of the Ad Hoc Committee, November 12, 1964, in *The Berkeley Student Revolt,* p. 567
176   Cited by Draper, *op. cit.,* p. 41
177   Cited in "Chronology . . . ," *op. cit.,* p. 118
178   *Ibid.,* p. 130
179   Cited by Draper, *op. cit.,* p. 92
179   Draper, *op. cit.,* p. 94
179   Cited by Draper, *op. cit.,* p. 97
180   Cited by Draper, *op. cit.,* p. 98
181   Cited in "Chronology . . .," *op. cit.,* pp. 178 and 179
182   Cited in "Chronology . . .," *op. cit.,* p. 182 and p. 194
183–184   Anatol Rapoport, "Dialogue of Monologue," in *Teach-Ins: U.S.A.,* ed. by Louis Menashe and Ronald Radosh (Praeger, 1967)
184   Roger Rapoport, "Protest, Learning, Heckling Spark Viet Rally," in the *Michigan Daily* (March 26, 1965), reprinted in *Teach-Ins: U.S.A.*
184   Arnold S. Kaufman, "Teach-Ins: New Force for the Times," in *The Nation* (June 21, 1965), reprinted in *Teach-Ins: U.S.A.*
184   Joan Wallach Scott, "The Teach-in . . .," in *Studies on the Left* (Vol. V No. 3, 1965), reprinted in *Teach-Ins: U.S.A.*
185   Cited in *Facts on File* (1968), p. 529
186   *Crisis at Columbia,* (The Cox Commission Report) (Vintage, 1968), p. 11
187   Cited in *Crisis at Columbia,* p. 206
188   *Ibid.,* p. 68
190–191   Cited by Evert Clark in *The New York Times* (April 23, 1968)
192   *Facts on File* (1969), p. 231
193   Cited by Michael T. Kaufman in *The New York Times* (May 14, 1969)
195   The Vine City Project Paper on "Whites in the Movement," cited in *The New Student Left,* ed. by Mitchell Cohen and Dennis Hale (Beacon, 1967), p. 100
196   *Ibid.,* pp. 99–100 and p. 103
197   *Facts on File* (1966), p. 140
198   *The New York Times* (March 24, 1968)
198   David Nolan in the *Guardian* (May 10, 1969)

200	*Facts on File* (1968), p. 150
200	*The New York Times* (March 22, 1968)
200	Thomas A. Johnson in *The New York Times* (Nov. 15, 1968)
200	C. Gerald Fraser in *The New York Times* (May 9, 1969)
201	Nathan Hare, cited by M. A. Farber in *The New York Times* (Jan. 16, 1969)
202	*The New York Times* (May 8, 1969)
202	*Facts on File* (1968), p. 212
202	*The New York Times* (May 4, 1968)
205	*The New York Times* (Feb. 15, 1969)
207	David F. Rosenbaum in *The New York Times* (May 18, 1969)
208	Paul Hofmann in *The New York Times* (April 14, 1968)
208	*The New York Times* (July 2, 1968)
210	Robert A. Haber, "From Protest to Radicalism: An Appraisal of the Student Movement, 1960," in *The New Student Left,* p. 40
213	Seymour Martin Lipset and Philip G. Altbach, "Student Politics and Higher Education in the United States," in *Student Politics,* ed. by Seymour Martin Lipset (Basic Books, 1967), p. 216
213	Keniston, *op. cit.,* p. 338
214	*Ibid.,* p. 337
214–215	*Crisis at Columbia,* p. 190
216	Cited by Raskin, *op. cit.,* p. 425
217	Mario Savio, "The Uncertain Future of the Multiversity," in *Harper's* (October, 1966)
217	Michael T. Kaufman in *The New York Times* (May 14, 1969)
217–218	Cited in *The New Student Left,* pp. 217 and 218
218	Mark Rudd, "We Want Revolution," in the *Saturday Evening Post* (Sept. 21, 1968)
219	Thomas Hayden, "Student Social Action: From Liberation to Community," in *The New Student Left,* p. 285
219	Cited by Robert Reinhold, in *The New York Times* (April 25, 1969)
219	Joel R. Kramer, "What Student Power Means," in *The New York Times Magazine* (May 26, 1968)
220	*The New York Times* (Oct. 6, 1968)
220	Fred M. Hechinger in *The New York Times* (May 11, 1968)
220	Robert Reinhold in *The New York Times* (April 23, 1969)
221	*The New York Times* (May 8, 1969)
221–222	Weinberg, *op. cit.,* p. 185
222	Mario Savio, "An End to History," in *Humanity* (December, 1964) reprinted in Draper, *op. cit.,* p. 179, and in *The Berkeley Student Revolt,* p. 216
222–223	*Crisis at Columbia,* pp. 34–35
223	*Ibid.,* p. 36, p. 49, and pp. 50–51 (three citations)
224	*Ibid.,* pp. 97–98
224	Cited in *Look* magazine (April 2, 1968)
225	Robert Schlesinger, Jr., "Joe College Is Dead," in the *Saturday Evening Post* (Sept. 21, 1968)
226	Seth S. King in *The New York Times* (April 25, 1969)
226	Cited by Peter Kihss in *The New York Times* (April 25, 1969)
226–227	Norman Cousins in the *Saturday Review* (May 18, 1968)
228–229	Bernard Weintraub in *The New York Times* (May 8, 1969)
229	John Kifner in *The New York Times* (May 11, 1969)
230	Theodore Hesburgh, address to National Catholic Educational Association convention in Detroit, cited by Gene Currivan in *The New York Times* (April 9, 1969)
232	George F. Kennan, "Rebels Without a Program," in *The New York Times Magazine* (Jan. 21, 1968)
232	Kerr, *op. cit.,* pp. 53–54
233	Rudolph, *op. cit.,* p. 491, and cited by Kerr, *op. cit.,* pp. 52–53
234–235	Taylor, address at Boulder, *loc. cit.*

INDEX

242